DEDICATION

Arcadia and Jake, you were my inspiration for this book.

I dedicate this book to the next generation of young professionals and believe that the brave actions you take each day will lead to the successful and fulfilling life you so deserve!

CONTENTS

Introduction　　　　　　　　　　　　　　　　　vii

1　How Not to Fail at Your First Job　　　　　　1

2　Why Self-Awareness Is the Key to Finding Your　10
　　Dream Job

3　Why Perfectionism Is Your Enemy　　　　　23

4　Imposter Syndrome, Competition, and Scarcity　31

5　Taking Risks, Trusting Your Gut, and Making Big　39
　　Decisions

6　Success Is an Inner Game　　　　　　　　52

7　How You Can Find Mentors, Build Your　　63
　　Professional Network, and Conduct Informational
　　Interviews

8　Interviewing Insights and Strategies　　　81

9　Time Management and Goal Setting　　　95

10　What Bosses Love　　　　　　　　　　105

11　Tips for Managing Your Well-Being　　　115

12　The Secret to Living Is Giving　　　　　126

Afterword　　　　　　　　　　　　　　　133

Acknowledgements　　　　　　　　　　135

About the Author　　　　　　　　　　　137

INTRODUCTION

Finding your dream job and creating a fulfilling life has two parts to it. In this book I will cover both: the "how to" part and the "how to overcome our inner fear" part that stops you from taking action. Most career guides focus solely on the *easy* part; they teach you things you need to do: network and interview effectively. But you and I know that there's a big difference between knowing what you need to do to land that job, and actually doing it!

What's different about this book is that it focuses on the *hard* part of success — managing our own minds, which are fear-generating, problem-finding machines. I will provide you with insights and strategies so you can feel in control of your career and take brave action every day, even in uncertain times. In this book, you will learn why success is an inner game and how you can create the successful and fulfilling career you deserve.

I'm Eva Wisnik, President and Founder of Wisnik Career Enterprises Inc., a corporate search firm for law firms, consulting companies, and financial institutions. I've spent my career hiring and placing thousands of professionals into top firms across the country, and in this book, I share the secrets to success that you can't and won't learn in school.

Prior to starting my own company 25 years ago, I spearheaded talent acquisition for major law firms and investment banks. I've made it my life's work to help professionals navigate their careers, and I want to help you too.

I chose to write this book in the middle of a pandemic because our world is characterized by uncertainty, and it is your generation that I believe can change it for the better. As a mother to two college kids trying to navigate their own career paths, I understand the extraordinary obstacles resulting from the current state of our world.

Although there are challenges, I believe none are too big to overcome. I will show you how to understand your unique talents and how to present yourself to the right employers as the excellent job candidate you are. This book will give you the information, insight, and inspiration you need to own your career and thrive! Consider me Your Fairy Job Mentor.

The biggest obstacles to finding a great job are not external — a challenging economy or competitive job market — but rather lie in overcoming our own fears! We all have a fear of failure, fear of being vulnerable, fear of asking for help, and sometimes even fear of success. Every achiever I have ever met worries that they're not good enough and that there's a shortage of good job opportunities for them. These are all Big Lies that I will come to shatter by the end of this book.

If you follow the advice in this book, you can land your dream job, and live a life of meaningful contribution and fulfillment.

I know you will accomplish so much, and I can't wait to hear about all your successes!

-Your Fairy Job Mentor

1 HOW NOT TO FAIL AT YOUR FIRST JOB

When I graduated from Barnard College in 1985, working on Wall Street was the thing to do. I interviewed on campus with several financial institutions and was offered three jobs. I picked European American Bank because it had a formal training program that sounded like a secure career track — plus, landing a job on Wall Street was something to be admired.

The role was highly coveted, and I remember my classmates being impressed that I was all set with a banking job right out of college. Feeling sure that my career was in place, I embarked on my post-graduation trip to Europe. Next on my agenda was having the right attire to play the role of a Wall Street professional. I was very excited when I found the perfect burgundy patent leather attaché case in Florence, right outside the Uffizi, to go with my three indistinguishable dark suits from Brooks Brothers. Of course, each was a skirt suit because this was the mid-'80s and professional women didn't wear pantsuits.

Every morning I took the 4 train to Wall Street and tried to blend in with the sea of blue suits as I walked to my office on Hanover Square. I felt very grown up hurrying to work with my *Wall Street Journal* tucked under my arm. I naively believed that if I had all the external trappings of a successful professional, I would be one.

Do You Have the Skills to Do the Job?

I hadn't thought too much about the actual skills required for the job, so I was nervous when I met my fellow trainees who'd attended less-elite schools but had studied business or accounting. The first few weeks were nice; we were wined and dined by the bank's leadership and told how we were chosen from a huge pool of applicants. I felt important and loved our Friday happy hour at Harry's on Hanover.

As fall began, it sunk in that for the first time in 16 years I wasn't going back to school. You know how if you're taking a class in college you hate, you can comfort yourself with the knowledge that the torture will be over in just a few weeks and a new semester will start? I realized this was no longer the case for me. By Thanksgiving, we trainees finished our accounting and finance classes with NYU business school professors, who came to our offices to teach us. But we didn't get to start a new schedule of classes: It was time for the real work to begin.

Our work consisted of analyzing companies' financial and accounting statements to determine whether the bank should lend them money. Staring at financial documents seven hours a day was painful for me. I would literally watch the clock and begin packing up my shiny attaché at 4:59 p.m.. My favorite part of the day was lunch, and you bet I took the entire hour even if it meant walking around the square to avoid returning to work one minute sooner than required. My feeling of dread grew each morning, when I had to return for another day of torture with no end in sight.

My lack of skills and interest in the work showed. I had a hard time staying focused during our Thursday morning meetings with the VP of lending and I began failing tests (yes, we had pop quizzes on interest rates and the newest Fed announcements). In February, less than a year after I'd graduated from college, the head of HR called me into a conference room and fired me.

The news was a crushing blow. I'd failed at my very first job. Me! The girl who studied hard, graduated from a prestigious college and did everything she was supposed to do. What went wrong?

A "Good" Education Doesn't Equal Success on the Job

My biggest mistake was that I believed one of the many Big Lies. This Big Lie, which is perpetrated by our society and often encouraged by our parents and guidance counselors, goes like this: Work hard, do well in school, get into a top college, and you will be set for life!

I did all that and then I fell flat on my face within months of starting my first "real" job because being a great student does not guarantee a great career. It's just one small part of what you need to do. When I reflect on that time now, I know I chose to work in banking not because I found it fascinating or because it aligned with my skills, but because I thought it offered me status and certainty. But as I quickly figured out, those are the wrong things on which to base career decisions,

I was far from alone. This is a lesson that many ambitious, high-performing students learn the hard way after college. *In writing this book I hope to help you gain the insights and skills you don't learn in school, but which you need in order to make the right career decisions.* I'm here to share tools and mentor you so that instead of chasing status and certainty, you can base your decisions on what internally motivates you and, as a result, find meaningful work that utilizes your unique talents.

How Focusing on Status and Certainty Can Hinder Your Career

At this point, you may be asking: *"What's wrong with prioritizing status and certainty?"*

When you prioritize status, you search for self-worth through external validation. For example, our obsession with attending the "best" schools is often a reflection of our need for *others* to perceive us as smart and successful. Status works as a short-term motivator, but it usually leaves us wondering, "Is this all there is?" Many of the attorneys I've interviewed have no idea why they went to law school other than to graduate with a prestigious degree. The problem is that achieving things for the sake of achievement itself will not keep you motivated in the long term. This results in getting trapped on the hamster wheel of success, working hard and moving fast without getting where you want to go, if anywhere at all. You'll end up making decisions that are wrong for you because your choices will be based on what someone else finds impressive rather than what you excel at or love.

Certainty is a big reason why many smart people choose a career in fields such as law, medicine, or finance. You might have heard others say that if you become a doctor, lawyer, or accountant, you will always have a job. We want a future that feels secure because we have a need for certainty, especially in our uncertain world. My father, an immigrant from a Communist country, desperately wanted me to be a doctor. He believed it would bring bragging rights (status) and supposedly ensure that I'd make a lot of money and always be employable. This is understandable, but it's misguided. If you have a passion for medicine, then you should go to medical school. I didn't, so it's a good thing I didn't follow that path. But clearly I wasn't immune to that need for certainty and status, because I let it guide me to Wall Street despite not having the skills for or interest in banking!

We all have a need for certainty. *But here's the insight: your greatest successes will come from your willingness to relinquish your desire to feel secure and to choose uncertainty instead.* It's like swinging on a high trapeze. You hold on tight because you're afraid to fall, but when you release and reach for the next rung, you can get to a better place than you ever imagined.

The Power of Welcoming Uncertainty and Taking Smart Risks

This is exactly what happened when I was 33 years old. I was working as the head of attorney recruiting for the oldest law firm in New York City, Cadwalader Wickersham & Taft, a job that offered me both prestige and security. I liked it and was great at it, but month by month my desire to start my own business grew. This desire scared me, because I had no savings, a 3-year-old child, and a husband who had just launched his own legal practice. What compelled me to take this leap was knowing that I was actually risking more by staying in my current position than I was by taking the chance on myself and starting a new business. If I'd stayed, I would've sacrificed the opportunity for even more success and fulfillment in my career. *Sometimes, things that look certain are in fact holding us back from our greatest potential.* Tony Robbins, who I spent a year studying with, says our ability to be uncomfortable and to trade in certainty for uncertainty directly impacts the quality of our lives.

Starting my own business was scary, but it was also the greatest career move. For more than 25 years I've been helping people find their dream jobs and build fulfilling careers. Over the course of my career I've hired and placed thousands of highly educated students and professionals into the country's top investment banks, law firms and consulting companies. In addition, I've gone on campus to recruit law students from schools such as Columbia, NYU, and Harvard, and I've watched many of them navigate careers from summer intern to partner. In the process, I have learned what the most fulfilled professionals do and I wrote this book to share these insights with you.

Sharing My Wisdom

Although I've worked with extremely high-achieving candidates from top schools, many of the most successful people I've placed did not go to top-tier schools or have the highest GPAs. I have also encountered many former outstanding students who excelled in college, but who felt completely lost a few years into their careers. Simply put, I've seen it all. It's been my life's work to study successful careers and learn what *really* puts a person on the path to success and fulfillment.

This work is my calling. I want to be **Your Fairy Job Mentor** and to share these secrets with you because you won't learn them in any school. I promise that if you listen to the advice I give and take action, you will pave the road to the successful and fulfilling career that you deserve.

If you've ever felt scared about your future and worried that there aren't enough good jobs out there, this book is for you. Whether you're a college student, a recent grad, or have been working for a number of years, I'll show you how you can have control over your career, find work you love, and flourish in every way. I'll light the path for you by sharing insights and the real secrets to a successful and fulfilling career and shattering the lies that are rampant in our status-obsessed culture.

Action Step

Let's start right now with a few moments of reflection.
Think about the accomplishments that you're most proud of today. Maybe you have a long list, or maybe there's only one thing you can think of. Either way, that's okay. Now choose one and consider: Was there a moment when you felt uncertain as to whether you would succeed, but you trusted your instinct and did it anyway? How did it feel to take that action? How does it feel now to think about it?

Taking smart risks is how you achieve your greatest potential. *What makes a risk smart is that although it's initially uncomfortable, your gut tells you that if you do it you will grow and learn.* When we take on these challenges, we develop new skills and overcome our fears. Smart risks are transformative in that *you* change in the process.

The gifts from taking on smart risks include: more confidence, resilience, and self-knowledge of your unique talents. So starting now, ask yourself *why* you're making whatever career decision you may be facing, whether big or small. Are you choosing something because it offers certainty and status or because you really want it and it offers you significant growth? I promise that if you start pursuing the path *you* really want and take smart risks, you'll take charge of your career and clear the path to the success and fulfilment you deserve.

Action Step

Use the following Accomplishment List and Efforts List to track all you do and keep yourself motivated!

Keeping Track of Your Accomplishments

Too often we focus on what we have yet to do and forget all that we have already accomplished so far. Use the space below to write down some of your recent accomplishments to keep yourself motivated!

1.

_____

2.

_____

3.

_____

4.

_____

5.

_____

6.

_____

7.

_____

8.

_____

Keeping Track of Your Efforts

Writing down exactly what we can do to accomplish our goals will only foster success. Use the space below to keep track of the efforts you can make to achieve your goals!

1. _____

2. _____

3. _____

4. _____

5. _____

6. _____

7. _____

8. _____

2 WHY SELF-AWARENESS IS THE KEY TO FINDING YOUR DREAM JOB

Shortly after I got fired from my first job, I decided to get an MBA. Like so many other young professionals, when our first jobs don't work out as planned or the economy is challenging, going back to school, something we know well and are good at, is the default. While I was studying for the GMAT and applying to business school, I took a temp job at a big New York law firm called Paul, Weiss to assist with the busy on-campus recruiting season. I instantly fell in love with recruiting. I liked all the planning and scheduling, and I easily memorized candidates' resumes and took a deep interest in who was interviewing them and whether they accepted their offers. To my amazement, I loved coming to work each day and couldn't believe I was getting paid to do something that made me so happy. Woohoo! I had found my calling!

When the temp role ended in January, I was hired for a permanent position as an MBA recruiting assistant for Lehman Brothers, a hundred-year-old investment bank. I was excited to continue my recruiting career, and Lehman Brothers offered tuition reimbursement — so I decided to enroll in a part-time MBA program at Fordham University. I was 24 years old and working for a very prestigious financial institution (this time in a role that played to my strengths), and I was attending business school two nights a week. I thought I'd figured out this whole career thing. There was just one problem.

What a Values Clash Looks Like

Have you ever joined a club or gone to a camp where you felt like you just didn't fit in — where everyone did or thought about things differently from you? That's how I felt at Lehman Brothers. My values were radically different from almost everyone around me and, as a result, I couldn't form a real connection to the organization or the people.

Let me give you a glimpse into the work environment at Lehman so you can better understand why it wasn't a good fit for me. When I joined the investment bank, our recruiting department was located on an actual trading floor. My boss was having an affair with the head of long-term bond trading. I knew this because I answered her phone each time it rang — it was 1987 and we had no email or mobile phones. Her husband, the head of equities, worked on the other end of our floor. I had to interact with all three of them every day, which was both stressful and disturbing.

One of my main responsibilities was to schedule traders to interview MBA candidates after the markets closed for the day at 4:00 p.m. The most frequent response I got when I approached a trader to ask if he could interview a candidate was, "Get the f%#k out of here!" I was living in *The Wolf of Wall Street*! I'd never thought of myself as a goody-two-shoes, but being immersed in an environment of cocaine, affairs, and verbal abuse made me feel like I didn't belong. These were *definitely* not my people.

But I tried to fit in anyway, because I loved my day-to-day responsibilities and knew that I wanted to build a career in recruitment. In addition to the tuition reimbursement Lehman Brothers offered, I liked the free lunches that were delivered to our desks each day at noon and the luxurious gym we could use before or after work, complete with personal trainers. I even joined in on the Hamptons summer house everyone on Wall Street just had to indulge in. I committed to a 1/8 share because as an assistant that's all I could afford. The house was in Hampton Bays, the least prestigious area "out East," with no pool and far from the beach. The four times I went out that summer, my bed was already occupied by people who were not "in" on the house and the heavy partying was more than I was used to. I didn't fit in with the crowd at my Hamptons share, but I did like going to clubs to dance to early Madonna and Janet Jackson songs. Each night ended with my many housemates piling into the Hampton Bays taxi van — the Managing Directors at our firm had warned us that DWI's were handed out like candy by police during the summer. They knew this because many of them had been pulled over while intoxicated.

The Hamptons share, the gym, the free lunches: These external trappings signified status and were easy to get caught up in. In some ways I wanted to fit in, but in many ways I didn't. Over our free lunches, the young women working as assistants to important executives on our corner of the trading floor would mention they couldn't pay down their overdrawn credit cards. As assistants we were making under $25,000 a year. They racked up debt to live in fancy apartments on the Upper West Side and get expensive haircuts at Vidal Sassoon. The manager who ran the summer program put her third Hermès scarf, a required accessory signifying you'd made it to the managerial ranks, on the company Amex because her personal card had been canceled. Glamorous perks are alluring, but I want to share these specifics with you to shine light on how easy it is to get caught up in status-seeking, to buy into an image, and to feel pressured to conform to a culture without stopping to ask if it's what you really want.

How a Culture Misfit Teaches Us Our "Musts"

The constant feeling that I didn't belong stayed with me throughout my tenure at Lehman Brothers, even though I loved using my skills to recruit the right talent from business schools like Duke's Fuqua, UVA's Darden, and UCLA. All these years later, I still remember how much I enjoyed planning and executing the on-campus interview process and summer program events. But I just didn't feel in sync with the company culture or my colleagues and supervisors. I couldn't ignore how my values clashed with most of the people I worked with.

Another value clash for me was how competitive and non-collaborative the work environment was. I still remember the chilling day in October 1987 when we experienced a major stock market crash. Traders were yelling at each other and the poor newly hired MBAs, who had started just weeks before looked shell-shocked. I understood this was a bad day for Lehman Brothers, but what I didn't expect was the level of fighting amongst senior leaders that went on for weeks afterwards. We could hear them screaming behind closed doors and it was clear that one group of traders was blaming the other for the big financial losses. The worst part came in early December, before bonuses were announced, when half of our recently hired MBA class was let go. They were as shocked as I was! The competitive work culture combined with how people behaved and treated each other, clearly clashed with my values.

Working at Lehman Brothers was a painful experience in many ways, but I want to share it with you so you can quickly spot bosses and work environments that may not be right for you. Our values are core to us, but we're often unaware of them until they're challenged. *Here's the insight: It's normal for your first few internships and jobs to feel uncomfortable. You can use these experiences to make wiser choices, because they help us figure out what we need in order to feel like we belong in our work environments.* Finding your people is not always easy, but it's definitely worth the effort to figure it out. Understanding your core values will help you to make the right career choices in the long term, and I'm here to help! This chapter concludes with a values assessment to help you begin identifying your work values.

While it can be hard to put your finger on what, exactly, makes any group of people "a fit," for you, it's important to drill down and understand what your "musts" are when it comes to your work values. After Lehman Brothers, I knew my skills were a fit for recruiting talent from top schools — *and* I learned that a company's culture had to be in sync with my values. I learned that my musts include a respectful work environment where the people I work with behave professionally and collaborate with each other. I know this sounds basic, but I didn't realize how much I needed these qualities until they were missing. Based on this new understanding of what kind of culture I needed in my workplace, and having had two negative experiences with Wall Street firms and one very positive one at a law firm, I decided to return to the legal field. I found a recruitment coordinator role at a growing law firm, Schulte Roth & Zabel, located in midtown Manhattan. Both the role and the firm were a match for my skills *and* my values. At Schulte, I would get promoted from coordinator to director over the next five years while completing my MBA in marketing. One plus for me was that the partners who'd founded the firm 20 years before I arrived were very entrepreneurial. They offered me lots of growth opportunities and welcomed my ideas. For most of my five years at SchulteI loved going to work every day, using my unique talents, and feeling aligned with the people and culture.

Invest in Discovering Your Values and Skills

There are many things you don't have control over when you're looking for an internship or your first few jobs out of college. But you do have control over how much time you invest in discovering your unique skills and values. Having this self-awareness is essential to your happiness and success. As you saw in my story about Lehman Brothers, it doesn't much matter that you can use your skills in a job if your values clash with the company's and the culture is a bad fit — you will be miserable. The sooner you get to know your own skills and values, the sooner you'll land a job where you can thrive *and* establish a career you love.

How many of your peers chose a college major solely because they thought they'd easily find a job and make a lot of money? I'm all for making a lot of money, but if you know yourself well, you can use your talents to find a career that is fulfilling, as well as lucrative. Most young professionals ask themselves, "How can I find a good job that pays well and has growth potential?" This is an externally focused question. The vital question they really should be asking themselves is, "What are my skills and values?"

Learn From My Mistakes

Let's go back to my first job out of college at the Wall Street bank. I took it because it paid well and I thought it would offer a stable career path with plenty of room to grow. Unfortunately, I didn't think beyond those things — and not only was I unhappy in the job, I also wasn't very good at it. When I accepted the role, I had no idea what the day-to-day work would look like. Once I began the training program, I found out that my cohort and I would be spending seven hours a day analyzing financial statements so we could eventually make lending decisions to businesses. Plus, we had an awful boss who created a competitive environment.

I failed at that job because I didn't know my own skills, values, and work style before I accepted it. Although I didn't succeed in the role, it was a huge learning opportunity for me to discover the type of work environment I *did* excel in and the skills I really wanted to contribute to earn my living. I found that I didn't have the quantitative skills to be a business analyst, that I was too extroverted to sit all day staring at financial documents, and that I wasn't motivated by competition with my peers. If I had done my homework on the responsibilities and, more importantly, myself, I wouldn't have taken the role.

Why Knowing Your Unique Talents Is Vital to Your Career Success

I promise that when you invest your time and effort into discovering your own unique strengths and values, you will have more control over your career. When you have clarity over your unique skills, values, and workstyle you can present what you will contribute to an organization and role with confidence. In addition, we can ask thoughtful questions to evaluate whether the culture will be a fit for our values. *The better you know yourself, the more control you will have over the job seeking process and the more likely you are to land a role that allows you to be successful.*

A skills assessment can help you identify both your innate skills and the ones you've developed in school. For example, if you're a natural planner, it's likely you've always planned out your study schedule and enjoyed coordinating events for your clubs. Skills you might have developed in school may include a high level of competency using Excel. I have found that most professionals' top skills surface early on. These core skills grow with experience and training, but they were usually apparent in middle school or high school.

Think about what you like to do when you have choice and the types of roles and responsibilities you gravitate towards. Are you a persuasive speaker who liked running for student government and giving speeches? Or have you enjoyed numbers and math from a young age and like to analyze data?

Although we can develop skills that don't come easily to us, I want you to focus on identifying three skills that are unique to you. *The insight here is: Don't make the mistake of thinking that if something is easy for you, it "doesn't count." Many people discount what comes naturally to them. It doesn't have to be hard to be valuable!* Your unique skills are your gifts. Knowing what they are and knowing how to communicate them to potential employers will be extremely helpful as you search for the right career.

Another self-knowledge piece that will help you to make good career decisions is having clarity over your workstyle. I've given the Myers-Briggs Type Indicator (MBTI) to more than 7,500 professionals since 1989. This Jungian-based personality assessment helps you know your preferred work style. For example, whether you prefer processing information internally or externally. It also helps you understand why you need to work in a structured environment or not. Some examples to ponder: Do you prefer to get clear about your thoughts by writing them down before discussing them, or do you get clearer about your thoughts after externally processing them with another person? Do you prefer to focus on one project or enjoy a variety of tasks daily? Do you like making decisions or generating options? Having clarity over your innate workstyle will help you to target work environments that will be in sync with your natural preferences.

What I love about the Myers-Briggs is that there is no good or bad way to be. The key is to know what your natural tendencies are so you can leverage them for the right work situations. I have seen this play out many times at work, both positively and negatively. Sitting in a room for hours looking at financial data and not interacting with people, which is what I did at my first job, was torture for me in part because I'm an extrovert and I need to work directly with people, not just information. On the other hand, the majority of attorneys I've worked with are introverts and prefer to research and write alone in their offices and then discuss the case with a team member or client once they're fully prepared. If you want to find out your Myers-Briggs type, you can find the assessment via a Google search or at mbtionline.com.

There are many things you may feel you don't have control over during your job search process, but knowing your unique skills, values, and workstyle are things you definitely do have control over. Invest the time to identify your unique talents so you can share them during interviews and easily showcase what you have to bring to the roles. This self-knowledge and clarity will make you stand out from peers who did not do their self-homework.

Knowing Your Weaknesses Is a Strength

Now that you know what your unique strengths are, I want you to identify what your weaknesses are. One of the Big Lies we're told is that we shouldn't have any weaknesses (at least, none that are relevant to our chosen field) — and if we do, we should hide them from potential employers.

We all have weaknesses. When you're clear about what yours are, you can choose to either strengthen them or find a career that doesn't require those competencies in large doses. For example, if you have off-the-charts math skills but you're not a great writer, you can focus on finding roles that don't require extensive writing, or you can work with a writing coach or take an online course to improve your writing. (Of course, you can also do both.)

Don't assume that somehow your weaknesses will morph into strengths just because you really want a particular job. If a role sounds appealing in every way but requires a skill or attribute you just don't have, you will show up each day feeling incompetent.

In order to be aware of your weaknesses, you have to release the belief that you should be great at everything. (We'll go more into this in chapter 3, which is all about perfectionism.) Struggling in pre-med classes and failing at my first job out of college made me very aware that hard sciences and analyzing financial data were neither natural skills for me nor ones I was internally motivated to master. There was nothing wrong *with* me; these were just areas that were wrong *for* me. I'm grateful for these experiences because they helped me discover what I was good at so I could build a successful career.

When you're identifying your weaknesses, one question you can ask yourself is, "What do I struggle with?" It's likely you've been taught that work *should* be excruciating. This is another Big Lie. Work can be challenging, but it should also be engaging and rewarding and it should play to your strengths.

This isn't to say you should altogether avoid work that requires you to use skills that aren't strong for you. There will be jobs for which you're naturally equipped with 80 percent of the necessary skills and are lacking in the rest. In this case, your job is to develop those weaker skills to the best of your ability, which requires discipline and commitment. Being a professional means you don't blow off the parts of your role that are tough.

Here's an example. One of my weaknesses is that I'm not

naturally organized or detail-oriented, but these skills are integral to the role of a recruiter. I had to work hard to develop these skills; I had to learn how to proof my recruiting reports and organize candidate files so all the information was easily accessible when the hiring committee was making an offer decision. To make sure I didn't miss important details, I read memos backwards in order to spot typos and double words, and I asked team members to proof final versions of reports for me before sharing them with the firm's partners. I used all my available resources and did everything I could to strengthen my weaknesses. I could only utilize these types of strategies because I was willing to be honest with myself about my weaknesses.

Now it's your turn. Be honest: Have you received feedback from a boss or professor about an area you need to improve? Is there a class of subject you worked hard at but still struggled with? Reflect on experiences you've had that revealed your weaknesses. Was there a time when you had to be a creative problem solver but your natural preference was to see things in black-and-white? Did you have a hard time staying engaged in literature classes because the metaphors sounded like major extrapolations to you? Did a volunteer gig requiring you to recruit others or solicit donations make you uncomfortable because you couldn't stand being "salesy"? Don't judge yourself for the weaknesses you identify in yourself. Just be curious about them and remember that self-awareness is the goal.

Once you've identified your weak spots (write them down on a list), decide how you want to handle each one. Which of these weaknesses are you motivated to strengthen and which ones do you want to avoid at all costs? Being honest with yourself will lead to a job that fits you best and ultimately to a rewarding and success-filled career. Instead of trying to make yourself fit into roles, I want you to find roles that fit your unique talents and where your weaknesses will not be major hindrances to success.

Let's wrap up this chapter with you writing down the top three skills you are excited to bring to a job, as well as the two work values that are musts for you. I also think it will be helpful for you to write down two competencies that you prefer to avoid in your future roles. Did this self-awareness exploration shed any new insights for you? I hope you are beginning to see a "picture" of what the ideal role would look like for you, in terms of what you would be doing and how the work environment would feel. In chapter 8, which focuses on interviewing, you will apply your clarity over your unique skills and values combination to present target employers with what you can contribute and this will make you stand out!

Skills Assessment

Rate each of the following on a scale of 1-10.
Which skills from the list below are you MOST
excited to use at work?

_____ Teamwork

_____ Online Research

_____ Writing

_____ Working with Numbers

_____ Computer Literacy

_____ Analyzing

_____ Strategizing

_____ Planning

_____ Organizing

_____ Time Management

_____ Innovating

_____ Selling

_____ Editing/Proofreading

_____ Customer Service

Work Values

Rate each of the following on a scale of 1-10. The environment you would be excited to contribute in is one that values...

_____ Helping Society/Others

_____ Creativity/Innovation

_____ Challenging Problems

_____ Collaboration/Teamwork

_____ Flexibility/Time Freedom

_____ High Earning Potential

_____ Siginificant Learning Opportunities

_____ Achievement/Recognition

_____ Diveristy

_____ Belonging

_____ Security/Stability

_____ Working in a welcoming environment

3 PERFECTIONISM IS YOUR ENEMY

One of the things I love most about what I do is that I get to work with super smart, ambitious people. I have learned so much not just from my clients, but from my company's interns as well. I've had the privilege of working with more than 50 interns at Wisnik Career Enterprises, all of whom have been highly intelligent and motivated to produce outstanding work. They teach me new technology and keep me up-to-date on the challenges facing young professionals.

Along with ambition and smarts, there's another trait many of my high-performing clients and interns have in common: a tendency towards perfectionism.

Another series of Big Lies tells us that if you're not perfect, you're a fraud and that you must stay at the top of your game (100 percent of the time) or your peers will grab the limited job opportunities and there won't be enough left for you. These lies perpetuate a vicious cycle of dangerous thought patterns that breed competition and will limit your success and fulfilment.

Many of us were raised to believe that our goal should be all A's — not just in school, but in every aspect of life. For example, we say, "He got a perfect 36 on the Math section of the ACT, but he only got a 33 on the English." We completely disregard that the average score for the 2 million students who take the assessment is 21 and that a score of 33 puts him in the 98th percentile! Why? Because high achievers and top students are trained from a young age that anything less than 100 percent is not good enough.

Can you see in this one example how damaging perfectionism is? It doesn't inspire us; it causes anxiety, warps our perceptions, and limits our growth.

If you don't allow yourself to be imperfect and make mistakes, you'll inhibit your own success. You will learn and grow the most when you stretch yourself — and that requires taking on challenges that are initially uncomfortable, challenges that, at first, are actually beyond your skill and knowledge level. Think about the achievements you're most proud of: Did you start out as an expert, or did you have to learn and master new territory?

I want to dive into a few specific ways that striving for perfection holds you back from success and happiness.

First, perfectionism causes you to play it safe and stay in your comfort zone. When you're afraid of failing (or just falling short of impeccable), it's just not worth it to take a risk. This might mean never taking an Art History class in college even though it fascinates you, just because you can't stomach the idea of maybe getting a B. Then, after college, it might mean staying with a job you have outgrown but are excelling at, in favor of leaving to pursue a new role where your success is not guaranteed. Before you know it, your comfort zone becomes a narrow, claustrophobic closet where you can't even stand up straight.

Another way perfectionism holds you back is by skewing your priorities when doing work. When you're obsessed with perfection, you're liable to turn in work products that are overdone and maybe even late. Back when I hired law students for top firms, I saw summer associates disappear for days after receiving their first legal assignments only to emerge with beautifully written 25-page documents that were too theoretical (and delivered too late) to be of value to the client. In my own office, I've seen brilliant students overthink projects and make them so complicated that they just weren't useful. One intern had a knack for transforming straightforward memo requests into unwieldy documents with impressive words no one used or knew. He was smart

24

and he wanted to be helpful, but his perfectionism tendencies kept him from contributing in a practical way.

Perfectionism Often Leads to Procrastination

That leads me to another thing I've frequently observed perfectionists struggle with: procrastination. I used to think my oldest son had a time management issue. But one day I saw him sitting in front of his computer for hours, staring at a blank screen. When I asked him what he was doing, he said he was waiting for the perfect words to come into his mind. This torturous writing process went on forever, until the fear of not completing the assignment overwhelmed his fear of not being perfect and he began writing furiously to get the words down. He repeated this panicked pattern often, and as you can guess, the writing usually happened between 2 and 5 a.m. And then, no surprise, he'd be exhausted the next day at school.

It may sound counterintuitive, but perfectionism is why some of the best students don't grow up to be the most successful professionals. Doing well in school is helpful, of course. But those glittering grades don't mean much in the workplace if you can't take appropriate action steps to complete work assignments on time. Obsessive perfectionism and an unwillingness to actively seek out new challenges will definitely limit your growth and success.

As you can imagine, hiring managers often tell me that a major job requirement is for their team members to deliver timely work products. This is vital because your work is oftentimes being used to advise clients and make business decisions. Understanding that these assignments have a different purpose than the papers you wrote for school is critical to your success. For example, in school if you stayed up all night to write that brilliant research-based paper, you would get an A if it was perfectly executed. At work, if you stay up all night and deliver an A product, but the client needed a response by 6 o'clock the previous night, you get an F. Your boss wants you to produce error-free, well-thought-out work that can be practically applied, not magnificent works of art that are late.

If you want to be successful at work, not just school, you need to learn how to assess when a work product has to be an A and when a solid B will get the job done. Developing this ability takes a bit of experience and time. What I recommend you do when you begin a new role is to show your supervisor early drafts or even outlines and ask if you're on the right track. Getting their feedback before you dive in will help you to gauge when you should turn in the assignment because you'll have an even better sense of what is needed. Remember: In the real world, progress trumps perfection.

The Dangers of Perfection

Getting early feedback and making adjustments as you go is empowering because it's proactive and productive — the opposite of obsessive perfectionism. The need to be perfect is what's known as a *negative driver*. Having a negative driver means you are motivated to avoid something painful, rather than achieve something joyful. Instead of feeling energized to achieve a positive reward, you act out of fear of a negative result, such as failure or shame.

Perfectionism also produces an all-or-nothing mindset ("Either I get an A or I fail the class"), which creates extreme pressure to excel and breeds anxiety. For example, I have a family member who went to an Ivy League school for undergrad and grad school. She tells her kids that if they don't get all A's in school, they will be failures. I doubt she's joking, because all four of her kids have bragged on social media about dubious "achievements" like getting by on three hours of sleep a night. Sleep deprivation is only one unhealthy behavior that often results from extreme pressure to excel and to be perfect. Skipping meals, eating junk food, running on caffeine (or other drugs), not making time to exercise, and more are all-too-common consequences. (Check out chapter 11 on Managing Your Well-being for more on this topic) Many people can keep up this unhealthy pattern when they're young and have energy to spare, but negative motivation is exhausting and ultimately unsustainable. I've seen this vicious all-or-nothing mindset lead to burnout for many professionals. When I've asked super achievers what motivates them, oftentimes the most accomplished ones have told me it's a fear of failure. Imagine getting out of bed each morning and working your butt off not to feel fulfilled, have fun, or create something meaningful, but just to avoid failure. No wonder so many high achievers are anxious and burn out! Being motivated by a negative driver like fear of failure results in an exhausting life, no matter how impressive your LinkedIn profile may be.

How to Remedy Perfectionistic Tendencies

How do you overcome your perfectionism? Start by acknowledging that perfection is rarely attainable and not healthy. How many of your peers got a perfect score on their ACTs or a perfect GPA? And if they did, what was the cost — not just financially, for tutors, but also health-wise, in terms of stress and lost sleep?

Another way to think about this is to reflect on a time when you or someone you know stayed up late to make revision after revision to a paper that was 90 percent complete at midnight. Those extra hours may have earned you an A instead of an A-minus, but was it worth the sleep deprivation, 3 a.m. junk food, and obsessive, anxiety-inducing wordsmithing? I've worked with dozens of perfectionistic students, and I always tell them the same thing: I'd much prefer you hand me solid B-plus work in half the time. Then we can tweak it together to make it A-worthy, or we might just choose to use the B-plus product because it's *good enough.*

To break your perfectionism, I suggest putting a sign over your computer that says **Progress, Not Perfection**! When you focus on actually getting things done well, rather than tormenting yourself trying to be perfect, you are likely to produce much better results with far less pain. *Having high standards and working hard are great traits.*

Expecting constant perfection from yourself is not!

If you could relate to that story about my son panic-writing essays in the middle of the night, this mantra of "Progress, Not Perfection" is especially important. When you find yourself staring at a blank screen, willing the exact right words to come forward, start with a rough outline instead. Break out sections, add bullets, and just start getting the words down before the fear of missing the deadline overwhelms you. Once you lower the stakes and just start writing without the need to be perfect, it's very likely that your words will flow. Save your brilliance for the editing part of the task. I've learned from professional writers that "writing is rewriting." There is no such thing as a perfect first draft. Writing is about going back over what you've got and making it better, bit by bit.

Why Perfectionists Have a Hard Time Making Decisions

Writing is not the only task that paralyzes perfectionists — they often have a hard time making decisions, too, because the fear of making the wrong decision overwhelms them. This is what's going on when the class valedictorian can't decide between two Ivy League schools and waits until 11:59 p.m. on April 30th to pick one. Then, four years later, she's in the same situation when trying to pick a career path. Many perfectionists even try to postpone the decision by earning multiple degrees. (By the way, once you have one master's degree, will another one make you more marketable or get you more pay? Unlikely.)

It's okay not to know precisely what your calling is when you're in your twenties. What will help you figure it out is trying different internships and jobs, even if this means making some wrong decisions and failing. I urge you to rethink what failure really looks like. I challenge you to consider the possibility that failure does not result in death, but growth. When you release your need to be perfect, you give yourself space to stretch far beyond your current capabilities.

28

Failure is a Great Teacher

When I study successful people and ask them what their greatest learning moments were, they often cite a time when they failed or had to deal with a big disappointment, like not getting into their first choice college or taking the wrong job. Yes, these experiences were painful when they occurred, but they forced the person to tap into their resilience and taught them things about who they were that they didn't know before. This is true for all of us. *Our failures are amazing teachers!* Instead of fearing them, I want you to see them as milestone opportunities to learn and to grow. When you take on new challenges such as internships in fields that are new to you, you will acquire new abilities and true confidence. You can then tap into that confidence the next time you find yourself in uncharted territory, reminding yourself, "I've done this before and I can do it again." Confidence, courage, the willingness to take smart risks, and resilience are what the most successful professionals have in common.

To conquer decision paralysis, I recommend you train yourself to make the best decision you can under the given circumstances. *Allow yourself the space to possibly make the wrong decision.* Yes, I said it's okay to make a wrong decision! There are legitimate reasons I want you to take the pressure off of trying to make the "one right decision" and instead make the best decision under the circumstances. First of all, if you make the wrong decision, you're not locked in for life. You get do-overs. If you don't like your first job out of school, as I didn't, you get to try again. If you don't like your college, you can transfer. Second, wrong decisions teach us who we are and what's really right for us. When we make a decision that results in a failure (such as when I chose to work on Wall Street), we can learn from that failure and get closer to what's right for us. In fact, you may want to eliminate the word *failure* from your vocabulary altogether and replace it with *learning opportunity*. When you make the best decision under the circumstances, you'll either succeed or you'll learn! Either way, that's a win.

I often tell my kids that when they are faced with a difficult decision that doesn't have a clear right or wrong answer, it's best to make a decision and then work hard to make it the right decision. For example, I have observed kids pick a college they were unsure about and then remain ambivalent about their choice for the next four years. Instead, they could have put all their energy into making that choice the best experience it could be.

Action Step

Think of a decision you have to make in the near future. What experiences from your past can you draw upon that will help you to make the best decision under these circumstances?

4 IMPOSTER SYNDROME, COMPETITION, AND SCARCITY

Perfectionism and Imposter Syndrome

I recently went for a walk with a neighbor (I'll call her Beth) who is both a mom and an endocrinologist. Over the course of our conversation, I learned that Beth didn't think it was a big deal that she was a published expert in her field ("Doesn't everyone do that?" she asked sincerely). A few days later, I was speaking with a past intern who is a junior at a prestigious college and currently has a 3.85 GPA (I'll call her Kayla). In a similar manner, Kayla assumed that her peers from high school were also excelling in college, so her GPA wasn't worth much.

Both women downplayed their achievements not just to be humble, but because they really believed they were easy for others to achieve. Not only that, but they also exaggerated both their peers' achievements and their own shortcomings. Beth told me that she feared that she wasn't as good a mom as other women in our town who didn't work the hours she did. Likewise, Kayla compared herself to one of her high school friends who attended an Ivy League university. She thought her friend was guaranteed to get into a top law school but didn't think she had a shot.

What came up in both of these conversations was all too

familiar: Beth and Kayla both suffered from imposter syndrome.

Imposter syndrome is a thought pattern where high-achieving individuals doubt their accomplishments and fear being exposed as a fraud. I see it a lot among students and professionals who strive to be perfect and frequently compare themselves to others. A 2019 Brigham Young University study showed that imposter syndrome is not uncommon among high achievers. Researchers interviewed students in an elite academic program and found that 20 percent of them suffered from *very strong* feelings of inadequacy.

Perfectionism often goes hand-in-hand with imposter syndrome because when you expect yourself to constantly perform at an extremely high level, you tend to view even small challenges and "failures" as significant. For example, if you took several APs in high school you might still beat yourself up for only getting a 3 on the microeconomics exam because, in your mind, you didn't study enough. Or maybe you still feel insecure about the fact that you only got accepted to two of five elite colleges, even though you ended up at a school you love. Because you expect perfection, every time you fall short of it you give yourself cause to question just how smart you *really* are.

People suffering from imposter syndrome hold themselves to impossibly high standards and therefore have distorted images of themselves. While others see them as successful, smart, and so on, they think they're frauds. They dismiss their own accomplishments and exaggerate their shortcomings. And they're afraid they'll be "found out" if they *ever* make a mistake. Sadly, I have heard this from more than a few of the most admired and accomplished professionals I know well. My gut tells me that this occurs in part because these high achievers have relied on external validation, such as attending elite schools, earning perfect grades, and working for prestigious companies, for their sense of worth. They lack the internal belief that they are good enough, despite all they have achieved.

Ways to Conquer Imposter Syndrome

By trashing the Big Lies you've grown up with and instead developing the self-knowledge and mindset to take brave career actions based on what is right *for you*, you will cultivate a sense of self-worth that isn't tied to external validation. Learning to trust yourself and to make career decisions you feel good about, not just ones that look good on your resume, will help you build confidence that is rooted in knowing that you are good enough, no matter what happens externally. This includes not getting an internship or what you think is your dream job. As you put yourself out there and take brave action, I encourage you to adopt this mantra: *There are no failures, just opportunities to learn and grow.*

To achieve this vital inner validation where you don't tie your self-worth to external accomplishments, you must retrain yourself to believe that competition and perfectionism are your enemies. *To feel truly successful inside, you must begin trusting yourself to take smart risks and build confidence that empowers you to deal with external challenges that will come along — like a pandemic or an uncertain economy.*

Why do so many high achievers have low self-confidence? Why do so many of them not let their incredible achievements really sink in? I think it's because they have come to believe that if they do, they'll lose their motivation. They were raised not to get a swollen head just because they did well in school and to always remember that there are many students who are smarter than them. *I appreciate parents' sincere desire to keep their kids grounded, but I've come to believe that by taking stock of our achievements and recognizing our unique gifts we will grow that internal knowing that we are good enough and our achievements were not just luck.* Instead of developing a big ego, doing this gives us confidence and clarity as to what our strengths are and makes us eager to contribute even more.

To build up evidence of everything you do well and to encourage you to take brave action, I suggest you keep an **Accomplishments List** in your phone where you write down every accomplishment: Every time you're accepted to a school, club, or team; every good grade you earn; every time you solve a tough problem or learn a new skill. Include non-school accomplishments, too, such as being promoted at your part-time job or learning to play a new sport. Instead of developing a big ego, keeping an Accomplishments List gives us confidence and clarity as to what our strengths are and makes us eager to contribute even more.

I also want you to have another list easily accessible in your phone. Call this one **Efforts List.** This is where you can write down each time you did something uncomfortable, like sending a LinkedIn note to an alum asking if you could speak to them about their field, or volunteering to take on a work assignment that is outside of your comfort zone. When my oldest son attended boarding school for eighth and ninth grades, teachers gave students two grades: One was based on how they performed in the class and the other reflected how hard they worked and how much effort they put in. Sometimes when we do well in a subject because it comes naturally to us, we may discount our unique talent in this area. We think, "Math comes easily to me so it doesn't mean I'm that smart." (Of course, we do the opposite, too! If we study every night for math class, we often tell ourselves, "I only do well because I put in so much work. I'm not actually smart.")

This kind of thinking undermines our sense of self-worth and fuels our imposter syndrome. But once we track ALL the things we do well, which could include things like working out five times a week for a month or applying to seven internships each week there will be overwhelming evidence to show us our many unique talents and good habits, and we will be less likely to discount them. *Monitoring the effort you put into taking brave actions will help fuel your self-confidence because you will see how your initiatives generate results you want.* You will feel more in control of your life no matter what the external challenges are.

Don't Make Competition and Scarcity Your Problem

One of the main drivers for competitive thinking is the fear of scarcity — that there's a shortage of desired resources and opportunities, including jobs. The fear that there aren't enough jobs to go around skyrockets during times of uncertainty, such as during a pandemic and especially when the economy is strained.

If you have a tendency toward perfectionism, chances are you've also seen yourself as being in competition with your peers since at least high school. You competed for everything from class rank and admission to top college to spots on varsity teams and student government positions. You've been trained to believe that opportunities are scarce and must be ruthlessly fought for. I want to destroy the erroneous belief that there's so much competition that it's impossible to get a position, even in challenging times. Living this Big Lie needs to end with you! I don't want you to live in fear that you are not enough and there's not enough for you out there.

Our competitive fears are often triggered when we compare ourselves to our peers with similar credentials and desires, and when we believe what we want is limited. Competition can be healthy and motivating (for example, if you and your friend are competitive about your tennis skills, that friendly rivalry can make you both better players). But all too often it becomes an obsession and instills a scarcity mentality.

When you live with a competitive mindset, your sense of security and success is always dependent on who "won." You start to see life as a zero-sum game and believe that another person's success equals your failure. For example, even if you got a short-term thrill from getting into a college that another top student in your high school didn't get into, you'll eventually find someone who got into a college you were rejected from, or who earned a merit scholarship you didn't. *When you live with a competitive mindset, you will always find people in your cohort who are smarter or better at [fill in the blank] than you are.* It's a no-win game. Inevitably,

35

competing with your peers will make you feel that you're not enough and will undermine your confidence.

The Competitive Job Market Should NOT Be Your Main Concern!

I want to dispel another Big Lie: That there is a lack of job opportunities for you even in a down economy. I say this because every day there are young professionals who are landing jobs. The truth is that they don't necessarily have better credentials or more experience than you do. Instead of wasting time fretting over how competitive the job market is, they use their time to find jobs to apply to, and then they apply to many and prepare thoroughly in order to speak about what they can contribute to the role and company. Here's the insight: *The limited job market is not your problem. Your problem is in psyching yourself out by obsessing about the competition and playing into the scarcity mindset that there are not enough jobs.*

Here's one example. For my podcast, Big Lies Shattered, I talked to a recent college grad named Ben. Ben had to rethink his career goals when Broadway shut down because of COVID-19. He told me how he pivoted and decided to take a two-path approach to finding his first permanent role out of college. He decided to focus on jobs in which he could use his psychology degree and others that could benefit from his marketing internships. Ben identified open roles every day using job search tools like LinkedIn. Some days he applied to eight new openings, while other days it was as many as 30. Most of the jobs he applied to he never heard back from, but he was committed to the process of applying. I want to underscore that Ben treated applying to jobs like a job itself. He focused on applying to as many as possible that fit his criteria and did not waste his energy on guessing who his competition was. His effort paid off: Ben ended up with two great offers, and he chose a position in a mental health clinic. Check out Big Lies Shattered podcast accessible on our website www.YourFairyJobMentor.com

Here's another success story. Ameerah, a college junior I

interviewed for the podcast, landed a summer internship in investment banking right in the middle of the pandemic. When I asked her to share her process for securing this highly coveted internship, she said she applied to more than 100 roles over six months and received 60 rejections before even getting an initial interview. Even once she started getting call-back interviews, she didn't stop applying. When Ameera was wait-listed for her top choice summer role, she still pursued new roles. This is what perseverance looks like! Instead of worrying about her competition and the scarcity of internships for college students, she focused on what she had control over, which was finding available internships at financial institutions and being prepared for her interviews. This was her "secret" to landing her dream summer internship! *(Check out our Big Lies Shattered podcast on all major platforms)*

Ben and Ameera kept up their momentum and internal motivation by focusing on what they could control: applying for as many roles as they could identify and showing up prepared when offered an interview. Focusing on their competition would have only distracted them — and the same is true for you.

You have no control over the backgrounds of other people applying for the same role. If you do find out that they have a higher GPA or more experience than you, you're likely to distract yourself with thoughts about how they're more qualified, instead of focusing on preparing for the interview with examples of what you learned and are eager to bring to the role. The bottom line is that it's a waste of your energy to preoccupy yourself with your "competition" when looking for a new role. I've conducted many interviews, and the candidate with the best resume does not necessarily land the role. If you want to get the job, focus on sharing what unique talents you have to offer and why you want the role.

You've Got This, Just Focus On What You Can Control!

Focusing on what you can control and recognizing your accomplishments are the keys to overcoming perfectionism, imposter syndrome, and fear of scarcity and competition. When we're obsessed with being perfect, we hold ourselves to impossible standards because we're so afraid of failing. When we have a perfectionist mindset, it doesn't matter how much we achieve or how hard we work. *It's never good enough.* The need to be perfect prevents us from learning and acquiring real confidence.

If you release your (unrealistic) desire to be perfect and trade it in for a desire to learn and grow, you will give yourself the space to try things and make decisions that may not always work out as intended, but that will have other benefits. You'll also take the pressure off, so you can hand in that paper or deliver that work project without being fueled by fear and anxiety. *If you release the limiting belief that perfectionism is attainable, what actually will be much more attainable is the success you desire.*

5 TAKING RISKS, TRUSTING YOUR GUT, AND MAKING BIG DECISIONS

Oftentimes our greatest growth comes from putting ourselves in uncomfortable situations. But our achievement-focused society tells us that if we study hard and get a good education, we can somehow bypass the whole risk-taking thing altogether. One of the Big Lies preaches that as long as we're armed with great diplomas, we're safe from having to take chances and possibly failing.

My dad, who had always owned retail businesses — first a candy store and later a car wash — was shocked when I quit my high-paying and prestigious legal recruiting job to start my own business. As a refugee who bravely brought his family to America to live a better life, he wanted me to be well-educated and not to have to take risks the way he had to every day. He wanted me to be secure, which to him (and many, many others) looked like working for a well-established institution with great pay and benefits. In my calculation, this business was needed (and had an existing client base), and *not* starting it was actually the bigger risk in that I'd be denying my own dream out of fear of failure. But I was afraid that my dad's fear would sway me in my moment of courage, so I didn't tell him for months. (Twenty-five years later, I can tell you the risk was definitely worth taking!)

Taking well-thought-out risks and putting yourself in uncomfortable situations pays off because you're forced to learn new skills and conquer your fears. For example, if you take a class that's out of your comfort zone (let's say computer science), and you struggle but master new skills and gain confidence in your ability to code, you'll know that you can start from scratch with a skill and learn something completely new. The same can be true if you apply for an internship in a field you have no background in (e.g. real estate) and allow yourself to feel way out of your comfort zone in the beginning. A few months later, you'll have had humongous growth in terms of your knowledge and confidence. Every time you take a smart risk and try something new and uncomfortable, you build up proof that you're capable of more than you initially believed .

You Will Never Feel 100% Ready

The idea that you're supposed to be completely ready before pursuing new challenges is another major myth. There's no such thing as being completely ready! No matter how hard you study or how many trainings you attend, there will always be a moment when you have to jump in and feel vulnerable. An example of this could be going up to a guest speaker after a lecture at your school and asking a follow-up question or introducing yourself. *The next time you're considering pursuing something new to you and you get that uncomfortable feeling in the pit of your stomach, welcome it. I want you to associate that feeling with the opportunity for growth!*

It's important to establish these thoughts and habits now, because discomfort doesn't ever go away for good. Even very successful and seasoned professionals have moments when they enter new territory and feel unprepared. There are two things I recommend you do when you feel unready. First, **tap into your resources**, whether that's a classmate or colleague who has experience in the area or your ever-present friend, Google. Seriously! Often when I ask our interns how they figured out how to do something new, like add a graphic to a client presentation or generate specific data using Excel for one of our salary surveys, they say, "I Googled it."

Second, **fake it till you make it!** The most successful people use this strategy when faced with things they don't know a lot about. "Faking it" just means tapping into your memory for prior situations in which you were faced with new challenges and felt unprepared and reminding yourself that you succeeded. Think back on that computer science class or that real estate internship. Get into that "I'll figure this out" mindset and start taking action. Of course, I recommend you use your judgment to determine whether this strategy is the right one. If you're doing an assignment for an employer and really have no idea what to do or where to start, ask for help. If you do have a clue, but you feel some fear as to whether you can get an "A," then just go for it!

Getting comfortable with taking smart risks is like building a muscle — you have to exercise it regularly. The way to do this is to be on the lookout for opportunities. *Successful people have developed an aptitude for spotting growth opportunities and acting on them without tons of inner debate.* An example of a "risky" opportunity for major growth that's easily available to students is public speaking. Choose classes that require you to give presentations, run for an office that involves giving speeches, or take on leadership roles in clubs so you get used to running meetings. Before you conclude that these things simply aren't of interest to you, I want you to sense that uncomfortable feeling in your body. This is exactly what a growth opportunity feels like! By embracing that feeling instead of running from it, you'll strengthen your skills and confidence and, as a result, have more control over your success.

If you're currently working and want to develop your public speaking skills, there are two things you can do. First, seize opportunities to speak at department meetings or even on Zoom calls. When your manager asks, "Does anyone want to look into this?" raise your hand and say, "I will do some research and report back at our next meeting." This will afford you a chance to prepare, address your group with your findings, and practice your public speaking skills. My second recommendation is to join a Toastmasters International Group. I joined one when I was in my twenties. We met every Monday at 7 p.m. in a conference room in the MetLife Building in midtown Manhattan. Our group of 20 people came from a wide variety of fields, but we all shared the desire to improve our public speaking skills. Toastmasters provides an organized platform for practicing public speaking and getting feedback weekly. It was one of the best investments I made in myself and it gave me the confidence to present thousands of seminars to groups as large as 500-plus attendees.

You can also take inspiration from travel. If you've had the privilege of being able to travel, then you might already know that it's one of the best teachers for building risk tolerance because you encounter obstacles like plane cancellations, hostels that run out of rooms, or getting lost in a town where you don't know the language. These challenges force you to solve real problems in real time. Each time you troubleshoot your way out of a situation, you learn that you're capable of more than you first thought and you gain real confidence. And you don't have to fly across an ocean for this experience. Travel can mean going someplace by car, bus, or train, or it can just be a metaphor for putting yourself into a different space from what you're used to. For example, volunteering at a hospital even if you have a fear of blood, or writing an article for your company newsletter even if you haven't written anything since college, will require you to figure things out that are initially "foreign" to you. *By inserting yourself into situations that are out of your comfort zone and feel risky, you give yourself the chance to master new skills and overcome your fears.*

Here's an example. When my two youngest kids were in high school, they asked my husband and me if they could be exchange students and study in Europe for a year. At first we were hesitant. One college counselor advised against it because it would mean that our daughter couldn't take the ACT during her junior year or take enough APs to be desirable to Ivy League schools. Our kids decided to follow their gut and went to Spain and France for the year. They lived with host families and were immersed in foreign languages and cultures. The first few months were rough! They could barely communicate with their families, and taking classes like environmental science and European history in other languages was incredibly challenging. But after a few months, life and learning became rewarding. The grit and resilience they built during that challenge-filled year abroad when they were 15 and 16 years old has had ripple effects that I still see today. I remember the summer they returned, they were working for their dad delivering closing documents to law firms throughout Manhattan. I asked them if they were comfortable getting around the city and taking the subway (they grew up in the suburbs and did not have experience navigating the city alone), and their response was, "What could be so difficult when everyone speaks English?" Their risk tolerance had increased because they had a new perspective on what challenges looked like and the confidence to overcome them.

You will build grit and resilience when you insert yourself into circumstances that initially feel beyond your abilities. This is why the most successful professionals frequently put themselves into uncomfortable situations, like training to run a marathon or volunteering for a project outside of their area of expertise. They proactively look for and take on new challenges even if they feel "unready" and know they're likely to struggle in the beginning. They have trained themselves to welcome challenges and have come to believe that the risks are worth it because they will either succeed or learn. These professionals grew their risk tolerance - and as a result have developed the courage and confidence to know that struggling and even failing will not destroy them. They have built a resilience mindset and you can too!

What challenges are available to you right now?

- Can you take a class that would require you to stretch and possibly struggle in an area you're really interested in?
- Can you run for office in a club or organization you are involved with?
- Can you ask your boss if you can take on a project that would be in a new area but would offer an

opportunity for you to learn something new?

These initiatives may feel risky at first, but by training yourself to see them as opportunities for growth and confidence building, you will be taking control of your career and proving that your greatest rewards come from taking smart risks.

Trusting Your Gut Instincts

I met Henry when he was a fourth-year associate at one of the most prestigious law firms in the world. He had attended Wharton and Harvard Law School and had graduated top of his class at both schools. Henry knew he wanted to leave law and go into business. He easily secured interviews with hedge funds and startups because of his outstanding credentials, yet he struggled to land a job because he couldn't convince savvy businesspeople *why* he wanted to join their company.

Henry had spent his whole life achieving things to "create options," but he didn't know what he really wanted. When he finally received two offers, one from a hedge fund and the other from a very promising startup, he had no idea which job was right for him. I asked him, "What does your gut tell you is the right choice?" He looked at me with confusion. Henry didn't have an answer, because every decision he'd ever made had been based on external factors. He was completely cut off from his gut instincts.

Despite his remarkable education, Henry was at a big disadvantage because he hadn't cultivated this important ability to connect to his gut instinct. *Being able to trust your gut and take courageous action even when you feel vulnerable is a major key to a successful career.* The idea that you can rely solely on your rational mind to make good career decisions is actually a Big Lie.

Over my three decades as a recruiter, I've observed that it's not the smartest students or those who attended the best schools who have exceeded their career goals: It's the ones who have been brave. It's the junior attorney who is willing to knock on a partner's door and ask if she can work on a deal she read about on the front page of *The Wall Street Journal*, or the new grad who calls a contact he met at an informational session to ask to meet for coffee and career advice. *It's not how much you know that results in success, it's what you do.*

In school, the most successful people excel at absorbing information. But in the career world, the most successful people share the ability to trust their instincts and take "massive action," even when it makes them feel vulnerable or uncomfortable. Learning how to connect to your gut instincts and act on them will be critical to your success.

Cultivate a Connection to Your Gut Intelligence

I believe that each of us is capable of cultivating a connection to our gut instincts. Even if, like Henry, you've cut yourself off from your gut, you can renew the connection and strengthen it. For example: Have you ever had an experience when something just didn't feel right, despite looking right "on paper"? Maybe you finished a job interview and just couldn't see yourself working for the organization because something felt *off*, even though it looked like a great opportunity based on the job description. You've likely had these experiences in your personal life, too. Think about those times when you read someone's social media profile and you immediately knew that you needed to meet them. Or have you ever walked into a room and immediately felt this group of people were not your people? That is your gut instinct speaking to you!

We learn to ignore these messages from our very smart and intuitive gut because we're getting competing messages at the same time: External pressures telling us how things "should be," not to mention our analytical mind telling us what the "right" thing to do is. When we ignore or can't access our gut intelligence, we are susceptible to making wrong decisions. Can you recall a time you took a class or said yes to a leadership role because your rational mind convinced you it would be good for your resume, even though something inside you was telling you not to do it?

This was your gut sending you sage advice. When you reflect on that decision now, would you do it again?

The professionals I've met who have the most rewarding careers trust their gut and take action based on its messages. *Training yourself to tap into your gut instinct and trusting that feeling will help you to make the best career and life decisions.*

I consider myself a rational thinker and very business-minded, but it's also true that I've made my best career decisions when I listened to my gut instincts. This was the case when I quit my well-paid and prestigious job to launch Wisnik Career Enterprises, Inc. Our gut offers a different kind of intelligence and insight from our analytical mind. You see, our mind is designed to protect us and keep us safe. *This is why our mind is always there: To put a spotlight on danger, real or imagined, and warn us of all the possible failures our actions may result in.* If you're solving a problem such as a math equation, your mind is a great tool. But if you're trying to decide what field to enter, your rational mind can get in the way. It may try to convince you to pursue jobs that offer a secure career track that look good on paper, even though you don't feel any excitement (in your body) and the thought of applying for jobs in this field fills you with dread.

Be Aware of Your Bossy Critical Mind

In addition to being loud and bossy, our mind is often critical, especially of ourselves. I sometimes refer to my mind as the trouble-finder. Because our mind is wired to keep us safe, it's vigilant about spotting (potential) problems. It's programmed to tell us what is wrong, not what is right. Imagine you have a "friend" who's always there to tell you everything that could go wrong if you take a particular path or make a particular decision. Add to it that they walk right up to you and speak in a loud, clear tone with lots of certainty in their voice. Now imagine you have another friend who always gives you spot-on advice, but hangs back and speaks in a soft voice. In fact, sometimes you really have to lean in to hear them clearly, but their insights are profound. This is what it's like to listen to your mind vs. your gut. It takes more effort (at first) to tune out the noise and hear what the gut is saying, but it's worth the effort. Now, I'm by no means saying that we should throw reason and analysis out the window and capriciously do whatever we want. We should pay attention to what our analytical mind warns us about and carefully consider potential consequences. *But when it comes to important decisions, such as which grad school to go to or city to live in post-college, we're missing out on very important information if we don't also tap into our body's intelligence.* Here's an example to illustrate the importance of body intelligence. Take a moment to think back to when you visited college campuses. Do you remember a school you visited that, rationally, was just as good as others on your list — it was ranked similarly and had the majors you were interested in, and so on — but after attending the information session and walking the campus, you just couldn't see yourself attending? It just didn't *feel right* for you? And was there a school you visited and as soon as you walked onto the campus you felt "tingles" and could see yourself there and that's where you ended up? Again, this was your gut instinct talking to you! It's always there and very willing to share valuable feedback. It's just that oftentimes we aren't listening. To access your gut instinct, you need to quiet down your mind, which can be loud and bossy, and ask your body what it feels is right for you. The more you ask and listen, the louder and clearer your gut messages will be.

Listen to Your Gut

If you want access to your gut instinct, pay attention and start to keep track of when you make important decisions that work out well. Did you use your gut instinct's input to arrive at your final determination? Conversely, when you made a choice and it didn't work out as well as you had hoped, did you ignore your gut and rely only on your rational mind?

I remember the moment when my gut instinct told me I had to write this book. In the back of my mind I always knew I would write a book, and each year I would ask myself "Is this the right time?" For several years my gut instinct would say, "Not yet." And, of course, my critical mind would loudly add, "You don't have anything meaningful to write about and it would take time away from your thriving business!"

Then on a warm summer day just after July 4th, right in the middle of the pandemic, my gut yelled out: "This is the right time for you to write that book!" This was no whisper! My gut instinct was so loud and clear that my rational mind was too stunned to come up with reasons why I shouldn't. My gut said: "Young professionals need your guidance in the midst of all this uncertainty. You love them and you can help them!" As will happen when your gut asserts itself clearly and profoundly, within days an online course appeared on how to write and publish a book and I dove right in! This course provided the structure I needed to outline the book and it led me to meet the best editor possible, who was instrumental in making the book a reality.

When you listen to your gut instincts and take brave actions, your life and career begin to evolve in a way that feels right and easy. There is another Big Lie we grow up believing: That things need to be hard in order for you to be successful, that nothing worth achieving comes easily. That's just BS! When you know what your gifts are and are ready to contribute them to help others, your gut instincts will guide you and assemble resources for you to accomplish your goals. You may be familiar with the famous line from Paulo Coelho's *The Alchemist*: "When you want something, all the universe conspires in helping you to achieve it." You can still use your analytical mind as a tool, but I highly recommend that you trust yourself to listen to and act on your gut instincts.

Making Big Decisions Is Easier Than You Think

Have you ever agonized over big life decisions such as

which colleges to apply to or where to live after graduation? It's easy to feel intimidated by these major choices, but they're actually easier to make than we initially believe. I'm not suggesting that you shouldn't do your research or explore your options. However, I have witnessed many times that once someone has done their homework and contemplated their options, they're usually left with one choice that is clearly right. The problem is that when the right choice is different from what they expected, they often have trouble accepting it.

When my daughter, Arcadia, was applying to colleges, she had her heart set on attending an Ivy League school. She was a top student in her high school class and her peers were all aiming for similar colleges. She applied early decision to Penn and was rejected. After working extremely hard in high school and to prepare for the ACTs, the rejection felt personal to her. It was a devastating moment, but one with a happy ending. After an exhausting college admissions process, Arcadia was offered sophomore acceptance to Cornell. She could attend any school she wanted her freshman year, and as long as she got a 3.3 GPA, she would be admitted to Cornell as a sophomore. It felt like a second-place prize, but, she figured, at least she would be able to graduate from an Ivy League school.

Arcadia had a number of acceptances from well-regarded state and private colleges as well as one non-traditional option, an American college in Madrid. Having spent an amazing year in Spain during high school, she thought, "If I can go anywhere next year, why not go to Spain?"

After her first semester in Spain, she came home for winter break and declared, "There's no way I can live in Ithaca!", where Cornell's campus is located. She realized that she loved going to a small school in a big city. The decision about whether to go to Cornell the next year made itself and she ended up staying in Madrid for her sophomore year. She got to participate in psychology research with a top professor and managed to visit 14 countries during her two-year stint in Europe before transferring to another small school in a big city: Barnard College, the women's college at Columbia University.

I share this story with you because when we're making big decisions about which school to attend or what career to pursue, we tend to put enormous pressure on ourselves and believe that we have to make the *one right* decision. We're told another one of the Big Lies that says the more we try to control these big decisions on our career path, the more likely we are to succeed.

But this is just not true. *When it comes to big decisions, we frequently have the right answer inside of us but it's buried deep beneath what we think we should do or others' expectations for us.* When we can access what we believe is right for us we get to own our lives. I want you to have this level of insight and inner trust over your big decisions. Let me share tools for how you can stop trying to control and start trusting your inner truth.

Tools to Help You Make Important Decisions

When I coach someone through an important decision, I do two things. First, I ask questions to help them uncover their truths. For example, I ask them what the worst-case scenario would be if they made a particular decision (or chose the other option). Identifying your fears or obstacles gives you the chance to actually address them, and it gives you perspective. This stops that "what if" downward spiral by anchoring you in reality. I also discuss their options in the event that the decision they make turns out to be the wrong one for them. For example, if they end up choosing a college that isn't the right fit or don't get accepted to their dream school out of high school, is transferring an option? The truth is there are very few game-over mistakes and many chances for do-overs!

The other thing I do is listen carefully as they talk, so I can determine what they intuitively believe is right for them. (There's the importance of connecting to your gut instinct again.) I believe that deep down inside we all know what's right for us, *especially* when it comes to big decisions, but accessing and trusting that instinct is often blocked by all the "shoulds." When I listen with my body and mind, I can often hear another person's truths as they speak. Their voice goes up a few octaves and their words flow when they access that part of themselves. They are no longer just speaking from their rational mind. It's one of the most rewarding parts of my role as a career mentor to witness this!

The next time you're making a big decision (or a smaller decision that has you agonizing), I urge you not to just make a pros and cons list, but also to listen to your gut. Yes, it's good to get clear on the facts of the matter. It can also be smart to consult others to make sure you're thinking about how your decision will impact your life. But I have observed over and over again that we usually know what's right for us when it comes to big decisions. The hardest part is hearing our gut instinct and trusting ourselves.

There are so many things we don't have control over. But if you really want to, you can develop a deep connection to your own inner knowing and trust yourself when it comes to big decisions.

The Limitation of a Pros and Cons List

Many Type A personalities default to creating a pros and cons list when making important decisions. This method has significant shortcomings. For example, I recently counseled a high achieving college student who had two consulting internship offers. After making a pros and cons list, we discussed which factors on the list would most likely lead to the best experience. It turned out what appeared most attractive on paper would result in less hands-on experience and mentoring. As we discussed this, it became clearer to her that what she valued in an internship experience was more than just prestige, but a company that would allow her to learn the most.

Hint: After making a pros and cons list, be sure to talk out the decision with someone who knows you and you trust. By doing this, you can uncover beyond your analytical mind what's right for you. Don't disregard your gut!

6 SUCCESS IS AN INNER GAME

I still remember clearly the week in September 2008 when my one-time employer, Lehman Brothers, filed for bankruptcy. This powerful financial institution was more than 100 years old, but within a matter of days it was closed for good. That was it — the end. Their debacle signified the beginning of what we now know as the financial crisis. The news shook me to the core as fear ran through all the cells in my body. If Lehman Brothers and many other banks could fail, how would my business survive?

The next several months were tough. Literally overnight my work phone stopped ringing. By summer, all my interview training programs were canceled and most firms were laying off the lawyers they'd worked so hard to recruit. It was a scary time, filled with anxiety and uncertainty. When the markets finally recovered, I vowed never to feel that kind of fear again. And what I learned in the decade since the recession put me in a very different position when the COVID-19 pandemic hit. I've been able to approach this challenge from a place of inner confidence. I know that I can contribute, grow, and be successful, even if I can't control external circumstances. I no longer wake up gripped by the fear I felt in 2008.

In fact, I have confidence that I will emerge more successful when this crisis is over. Instead of wasting my energy worrying about our clients needing recruitment services less — something I cannot control — I've chosen to see this time as an opportunity to write a book to help young professionals. I'm focusing on what I *can* control. I take massive action based on what my gut tells me is the right thing to do, and 90 percent of the time I feel confident that my contributions will reap success. Yes, I have moments in which my mind creates self-doubt, but I don't let these thoughts stop me. Instead, I have trained myself to override my fear mind and to take action.

Here's the secret: Success is an inner game.

In the 12 years between the start of the financial crisis and the onset of the COVID-19 crisis, I closely studied the works of experts and sages in psychology, philosophy, and spirituality. What I discovered and developed as a result was the ability to manage my mind. Today, I am keenly aware of when my mind is triggered by outside influences, especially other people's fear or the news. Or, when it just goes off on its own, especially in times of uncertainty, to spew self-criticism and fear. When this happens, I know how to confront and shut down these mind-generated self-destructive thoughts.

My mind did quite a job on me during the 2008 financial crisis; it convinced me that I had no control, that my business might fail, and that I was a victim of the failing economy. These were all Big Lies, but I believed them because I didn't know how to manage my mind. This time around, in the midst of a global pandemic *and* economic instability, my ability to manage my mind has enabled me to face the crisis from a place of confidence and *inner* certainty. I've been able to take positive actions that have helped me feel in control, and I've maintained a feeling of gratitude throughout these months. This is real success.

When we think of success, we tend to focus on what we will have when we finally get "there." The Big Lies tell us that we will feel successful when we have proven our worth by achieving outside validation. This expected validation may come in different forms: a graduate degree, a job with a prestigious firm, significant amounts of money in the bank. We think, "Once I have [fill in the blank], I'll be successful."

53

But I've met thousands of professionals who have amassed all this external "evidence" of success and still don't feel successful. Not only that, despite all their achievements, they feel a tremendous amount of fear when things outside of their control, like a bad economy or pandemic, hit.

The Secrets for Real Success

At this point in the book, I feel compelled to share with you what you need to know and do to achieve *real* success that is not dependent on external sources. A feeling of success that you have control over. As your Fairy Job Mentor, I believe that if you know this early in your career, you will have the tools and insights to fully embody your success, no matter how much uncertainty is happening in your world.

The most successful people know that real success is an inner game. They don't base their feelings of security, happiness, or satisfaction on a checklist of achievements or external circumstances. This is how I want you to feel.

The biggest challenger to your success isn't anything outside of you, not even a pandemic or a recession. It's your fear-generating trouble-finder mind that specializes in voicing everything that could go wrong — and everything that's "wrong" with you. *The hardest job we have, especially in uncertain times, is managing our inner critic.* Your inner critic is the voice that says things like, "Who do you think you are? You will never get that job. You're not as smart as him/her/them. Why would you even try and risk rejection?" Each time you hear this voice in your head, you **must** confront it and talk back. Forget the economy. Forget any lack of experience. *This* is your biggest career and life challenge. So let's talk about how to take it on!

The first step in confronting your inner critic is to listen to it. This voice can be sneaky, and at first you may think it's saying helpful things you need to hear. Your survival brain actually thinks it's being helpful and protecting you from disappointment and failure. In order to counter it effectively, you must become aware of how this ever-present foe undermines your confidence by making you question your ability to succeed.

How to Confront Your Inner Critic and Take Action

How can you tell when your inner critic is speaking up? Here are a few examples. When you're applying for jobs or to schools that are a stretch, your inner critic is the voice that says things like, "Are you sure you want to put in all this work just to get rejected? Focus on the safe options. If it's not a sure thing, it's not worth it." Or let's say you're thinking about running for president of a club you belong to. In this situation, your inner critic will pipe up to say, "The chances of winning are slim. So-and-so probably has it in the bag and you're really busy, anyway. Besides, imagine how embarrassing it would be to lose." It might sound like your inner critic has your back, that it's just offering helpful advice. *Don't be fooled: Your inner critic isn't your friend. It's poisoning your confidence by telling you you're not good enough, and it's undermining your ability to grow and succeed.*

Once you realize this fearful voice is not helpful to you, what's next? Simple: I recommend you tell it to f!#k off! I'm dead serious here. Although my inner critic has quieted down a lot over the years, it still pops up, especially during uncertain times or when I'm launching something new like my Big Lies Shattered podcast. It loves to say things like, "You're aiming too high. Yeah, you've been successful so far, but it's all about to come crashing down." As soon I hear my inner critic, I tell it to get lost! I remind myself of all the things I've accomplished that initially seemed unattainable, and then (step two) I take one action toward my new goal. Taking action is the most powerful way to shut down this voice. *Your inner critic is a bully, and when you confront it head-on and take brave action, it scampers away.*

The idea of "taking action" when you're being pummeled by your inner critic can seem overwhelming, but just remember that even *small actions* represent taking control, which weakens your inner critic's power. Taking action could look like making an appointment at your school's career center for a resume review or allocating 30 minutes a day to check out Handshake for new job listings.

The key is to focus on what you can control. If you're a senior in college and everyone's panicking about post-college jobs, you can excuse yourself from an anxiety-filled conversation and instead go research growing industries and find people on LinkedIn whom you can contact for informational interviews. Instead of standing by as your mind gets triggered by fear, you can take control by taking action.

By acting, you exert control over your life and generate the results you seek. The more you trust yourself, the more confident you become and the more willing you are to take courageous actions. Even if external things don't go as planned and setbacks occur, you have the inner confidence and resilience because deep down inside you know you will succeed.

I recommend you have a list of actions in your phone that you can take, and then act on one of them every time you start to feel fear or hear your inner critic tell you something like, "There are no jobs! And especially none for someone like you, who doesn't have the right experience." You will win this battle because if you take one action each time your inner critic acts up, not only will you shut this bully up, but you'll also start seeing results from your brave actions, which will fuel your confidence and get you closer to your goals. Think of this like Newton's First Law: An object in motion stays in motion. Once you start taking action, the easier it becomes to take more.

Confronting your inner critic is a lifelong commitment, but rest assured that it's something successful people do all the time. And it gets easier. Successful *people have trained themselves to actively listen for their inner critic and shut it down as soon as it starts spewing its toxic lies.* These professionals aren't fearless, they're courageous. They feel the fear their mind creates, but they forbid that fear to stop them from following their gut and taking action. They know success is an inner game and that managing their mind is the key!

The Danger of Loss, Less, and Never Thinking

Deploying the trouble-finding inner critic isn't the only way your mind undermines your confidence. It has another weapon, and it's called Loss, Less, and Never Thinking. This way of thinking magnifies challenges and disappointments and turns them into permanent blocks to success. Here are some examples of Loss, Less, and Never Thinking:

- You get a B+ in a college class and your mind tries to convince you this grade kills your chances of getting into a top law school. According to your mind, the **loss** is much greater than it actually is.
- You overhear your roommate tell a friend about an upcoming interview she secured. Your mind jumps at the opportunity to tell you you're **less** marketable than she is and frequently encourages you to compare yourself to her, making sure you always fall short.
- You get rejected from five consulting internships, so your mind tells you that you'll **never** get a role in consulting and advises you to pursue something less challenging.

We are all susceptible to Loss, Less, and Never Thinking. But we also have control over whether we choose to be triggered by these self-destructive thought patterns our mind generates. Again, the first step is to become aware of when your mind is sending you these negative messages. Remember, your mind actually believes it's protecting you from failure and disappointment, so it's easy to get tricked into thinking its "warnings" are sound. But once you catch on that the mind is making things up and actually has no evidence to substantiate its fears, you can clearly see what's happening.

Let's look at the third example from the list above. So you got rejected from five consulting firms. You still have control over finding more consulting jobs to apply to and spending your energy on taking action instead of beating yourself up.

Remember Ameera from chapter 4? She was rejected from 60 investment banking internships before landing her dream role. Managing her mind was absolutely essential to her perseverance and ultimate success!

The insight here is that even in the midst of major obstacles, we have more control over our careers and lives than we often believe. It's just that our mind can't generate creative options when it's hijacked by fear.

The Impact of Managing Your Mind

I'll be honest with you: Managing your mind can be really hard at times, but it's critical if you want to be successful and feel in control of your life even when external obstacles arise, which they will. And even though it can take a lot of effort and determination, managing your mind is vital. Otherwise, no matter how much you achieve externally, you will be plagued by your mind-generated fear and your inner critic will be there to tell you that you're really not that good and your success is temporary. That's why external trappings like fancy cars and corner offices don't actually result in feeling successful long-term. You can have all the stuff, all the titles, all the accolades in the world — but if you can't manage your mind, you'll still be driven by fear even decades into your career.

Vulnerability is a Superpower

One of the reasons managing your mind can be so difficult is summed up in one word: vulnerability. Our minds *hate* when we feel vulnerable and want to prevent it at all costs. *To our primitive survival mind, vulnerability equals death because it's a sign that we're in danger.* In prehistoric times, when vicious predators stalked us on the savanna, this instinct served us well. The problem is that even though we live in a radically different modern world now, our mind hasn't caught up. It can't distinguish between real, life-threatening danger and the uncomfortable feeling we experience when we ask for someone to help us with our job search. This might sound kind of silly, but it's true. And in fact, you can use the absurdity to your advantage. *When you feel vulnerable and afraid, mentally step back and ask yourself: Is this a lion-on-the-savanna situation or is my mind running wild?*

As I reflect on the thousands of achievers I have worked with, one thing is clear: They all shared a desire to *not* feel vulnerable. For example, most of the brilliant attorneys I've worked with despise business development because they hate feeling vulnerable and asking clients for business. They believe that classic Big Lie that if you work hard and go to great schools, you'll be set — and not need anyone to help you. I completely bought into this one! When I was in my twenties, I thought being successful meant that you weren't at anyone's mercy and that you were 100 percent independent. Boy, was I wrong!

I wish I could have told my 20-something self that life is much easier and more fulfilling when you are surrounded by people you trust and who have your back. Coming out of college, I really believed that if I landed a job I liked with growth potential, my life would be all set. Now I know that I cannot do anything meaningful and fulfilling without others' help. And even if I'd found a job early in my career that was great, things eventually would've changed and I likely would've needed to find another job... and then another one. I learned this lesson the hard way, but you can learn it the easy way right now: *You need others to help you.* The "I can do it myself mentality" is best left to 2-year-olds. Plus, keep in mind that businesses and markets change even if everyone is doing their job well. To feel in control over your life, you want to cultivate great professional relationships and have the skill set to pivot easily.

I now know that vulnerability is a superpower. Unlike in my twenties, when I equated success with being independent from others and not at anyone's mercy, today I know that I am most successful and secure when I'm *interdependent* on others. For example, I have trained myself to welcome the opportunity to ask clients for business because living in fear that there won't be enough new business is much more uncomfortable.

Let me ask you a question: What do you think will net you the best results: reaching out to a contact you met at an informational meeting on-campus to ask them if they can share your resume with HR at a media company you know has an opening, or submitting your resume through the company's online portal without asking for anyone's help? This is the kind of thing you have control over even in the middle of a pandemic. *The more you're willing to withstand the uncomfortable feeling of vulnerability, the more fully you will own your life and career.*

Success Is Not a Solo Venture

No matter how good a student you are, how hard you're willing to work, or how much you know, you will always need others' help. This might strike you as counterintuitive right now; after all, in school, asking for other people's help was often synonymous with cheating. We've all grown up in a culture that values independence and self-reliance. Vulnerability makes us feel weak, but it's time to debunk this Big Lie and embrace the power of vulnerability. Each time you ask others for help, you're demonstrating (and building) strength, resilience, and courage!

In studying the most successful professionals, I've learned that the ones in the safest positions are those who have strong professional relationships with people they can call in tough times (like when the economy crashes and they're unexpectedly out of work) or when they need help navigating an important career decision. As I look back on my 25 years of being in business, being great at my work is only part of what's enabled my success. Even more important? The amazing network I have created — and the fact that I am *unafraid* to ask my clients if I can help them with things like filling their job openings or presenting well-being programs for their firms.

You, too, can change your mindset around what it means to feel vulnerable and view it as a superpower that propels you to take action and build an incredible network of professionals who will be there for you when things don't turn out as planned. Yes, there will be times when you take brave action and the other person doesn't respond or says no. There have been many times when a client I've worked with extensively doesn't respond to a request for a meeting or isn't interested in my company's newest training program. To be honest, these disappointments don't impact me much anymore. For one, I don't take them personally — not every offer resonates with every person. Plus, for every client who doesn't respond or turns me down, there are three who say yes. If you make yourself vulnerable and build a strong network of trusted professionals you will have enough resources to feel safe no matter what's happening in the economy or how much uncertainty the world is experiencing.

Courageous Action Breeds Confidence

Most of us believe that you first need confidence in order to take courageous action. On its face, it sounds right — but I've actually found the opposite to be true. Each courageous action you take, even the ones that don't work out as you had hoped, build your confidence. Your confidence will grow every time you do something despite feeling uncomfortable. Why? Because instead of fearing these actions, you will rewire your brain to equate vulnerability with opportunity for growth. As you add up instances of taking action even when you feel uncomfortable, you'll build proof that doing so makes you more successful. Each challenge you overcome shows you what you're capable of, and this in turn grows your confidence. Your confidence will also strengthen because you'll become more resilient in the face of so-called failure. With experience, you'll come to understand that there is no failure, just learning and growth, and you'll become willing to take even more brave actions. Imagine being in a mental place where instead of viewing five rejections as a failure, you see it as a chance to take more brave action and you apply to 50 more internships and because you know that taking action, which is something you have control over, will land you a great role. This mindset is available to you! It's one you can cultivate starting right now, simply by taking action.

Success is an inner game, and I want you to feel confident and in control over your life no matter what is happening externally. If you practice putting yourself out there and overriding the fear you feel with the courage that lives inside you, you will be empowered to take the actions needed to achieve your goals and build the trusted relationships to create the successful career you so deserve!

What brave actions can you take this week? Remember if it feels uncomfortable, you're on the right track!

7 HOW YOU CAN FIND MENTORS, BUILD YOUR PROFESSIONAL NETWORK, AND CONDUCT INFORMATIONAL INTERVIEWS

If you want career control, establishing great professional relationships is key. Cultivating relationships with mentors, peers, and those you admire is a great investment of your time and something you have control over. But how exactly are you supposed to do this when you are just a student or recent grad? In this chapter I will share the steps you need to take to build a strong professional network.

The Do's and Don'ts of Finding Mentors

There's a Big Lie about mentors I want to shatter. The myth is that you just need to find one successful professional and he or she will scoop you up and take you to the top of the career ladder with them. I want to teach you how you can find mentors, as opposed to passively waiting and hoping one will find you. Many young professionals rely on formal mentoring programs organized by school, work or professional organizations to match them up with mentors. If you have that option great, but what if you and the mentor you are matched don't hit it off, or they are too busy to meet with you or they leave the organization? These are all real-life scenarios that I saw play out when I ran mentoring programs for newly hired young professionals. I want you to be well-prepared just in case...and I want you to consider assembling a number of **career advisors,** instead of one or two mentors to help guide your career.

Good news: You've probably already met some of your career advisors. For example, who wrote your letters of recommendation for college or served as your reference for an internship? Acknowledging who has already helped you succeed is a first step in recognizing and building these important relationships. Every time a professional takes the time to review your resume, coach you for an interview or provide insights about a specific company or career, they have acted as your career advisor. Your job is twofold: to **show appreciation** for their time and advice and to **stay in touch** with them. If you develop the habit of connecting with your career advisors four times a year when you *don't* need them, they will continue to be there when you *do* need them!

Before I dive into some tactics for initiating and maintaining career advisor relationships, let's go back to the Big Lie that you only get one mentor. Once again, you can learn from my mistakes! Not only did I have a bad experience with a mentor, but I also had a bad experience with a mentee. Fortunately, my struggles can work to your benefit. You'll see why making only one professional your mentor may not be the best strategy, and you'll learn what to avoid as a mentee.

Remember the story I shared in chapter 2 about how I finally found my dream job as a recruiting coordinator at Schulte Roth & Zabel? Well, I was placed there by a search firm, and the recruiter who helped me land the role, Christine, was someone I greatly admired. She was 10 years my senior, an attorney who had transitioned into headhunting and career development. I wanted her to be my mentor. Christine embodied the career I wanted to model. She'd earned a master's degree in counseling after practicing law at a prestigious law firm, and she spoke at our industry conferences and published articles on what lawyers needed to master to be successful.

Christine and I met for lunch every few months after she placed me, and I treasured her career knowledge and insights. Because she was well-known in our industry and had experiences in both recruitment and development, I wanted to learn from her. I had high hopes for our mentoring relationship and appreciated the time and advice she gave me as I embarked on my law firm recruitment career.

A year after she placed me, my boss left the firm and Christine placed our new director. Unfortunately, my new boss was the opposite of a mentor to me — she was actually my *tor*mentor. Barbara had been in law firm recruitment for 20-plus years and was clearly over it. She had no interest in working hard and she dumped a lot of her work on me, but she was quick to take credit during meetings with partners. She showed up late and left early, and she often said condescending things to me and made it clear that I shouldn't turn to her with questions. One of Barbara's go-to lines was that I had to "pay my dues," as she once had. I didn't mind working hard, but I really wanted to work for someone I could learn from, someone who was a good role model. Instead, Barbara made my life miserable.

I didn't blame the bad hiring fit on Christine, who placed her, but I was disappointed when I asked Christine how I should deal with Barbara and her response was that I needed to "suck it up" or leave. I was hoping for advice on how to navigate this difficult situation because I loved the firm and my job. Luckily, I worked for partners who valued hard work. They noticed Barbara's frequent absences and lack of adding value, and she was fired after a year.

Another red flag in my mentor relationship with Christine was when she sent the invoice for Barbara's placement fee directly to me. When I opened the envelope (remember, it was 1990 and mail was how information arrived!), I saw that my bad boss earned fully 100 percent more than I did. It was demoralizing to learn what she earned, and I was deeply disappointed in Christine's lack of judgment. This was the first time I began to seriously question whether Christine was the mentor I'd hoped she would be.

Later, the myth of having one mentor was shattered when Christine mishandled a sensitive situation with me. Over one of our lunches she encouraged me to interview for a more senior role at a competing law firm. I had just found out I was pregnant with my first child, but it was very early in my pregnancy and we decided the opportunity was worth exploring. This was my first interview since I'd arrived at Schulte three years earlier. I had an initial interview with HR and was invited back to meet with partners. Overall I thought it went well, but I didn't like the litigation partner, who interrogated me instead of interviewing me. I didn't hear back from Christine for a few weeks after this second round. My tummy was growing bigger and I felt compelled to tell her that I was pregnant because we supposedly had a trusting relationship. When I shared my news and asked her how to best handle the situation, she responded, "Well, that explains why you looked so 'dumpy' at the interview! They decided that although you could definitely do the job, you just didn't fit the image."

I wish I were making up this story. I'm sure my hormones were raging, but I burst into tears. It was beyond insensitive and unprofessional for her to say I looked dumpy. For three years I'd considered Christine my mentor, yet when I shared personal news that was both exciting and put me in a somewhat vulnerable position, she was rude and frankly mean.

Once I dried my tears and regained my composure, I realized I'd gained an important insight in that moment: I could admire and learn from many professionals, but I didn't want *one* mentor, because humans make mistakes and have lapses in judgment and may not be there when you need them. On that day, I chose to learn from and model aspects of different people's work styles and achievements. I focused on collecting multiple career advisors I could reach out to as I encountered new questions and challenges. This is the approach I recommend to you.

How to Be a Great Mentee

To build a collection of career advisors, you'll first need to master being a great mentee. This starts with proactively identifying professionals who can be good career (and life) advisors to you. As a great mentee, I encourage you to ask smart questions, listen carefully, and take thoughtful action based on what your career advisor has shared. For example, if you're thinking of applying to law school and your friend's mom is a successful attorney, you could seek her advice by asking questions like, "What do you wish someone had told you before you committed to law school?" and "What surprised you most in your first year of law school?" You could then follow up the conversation with a thank you note or email, recalling what you learned from her and how you plan on applying her advice. But don't stop there! Continue to stay in touch and update her on your career decisions, even if you decide not to go to law school.

Professionals you meet will be willing to make time to guide you if you make the effort to let them know that their advice is helpful to you. I know you may be thinking, "They're busy people. Won't I be bothering them?" No! The most successful people want to know they've invested their time well. By following up after your initial contact and staying in touch over time, you're demonstrating that their time is being well used. For example, I met with a number of people who had started their own businesses in the legal field before I launched my company. Twenty-five years later, I'm still in touch with one of those entrepreneurs. One of them, Neil, met me every few months during my first years in business and shared his insights on how to get big law firms as clients. I updated him regularly to let him know how my business was growing and even shared resources by introducing him to new contacts he could potentially do business with. It may surprise you right now, but over time you can become a career resource for your advisors.

I also want to share how one person I placed has been very effective at staying in touch with me and turning me into her career advisor. I met Ally a year after she graduated from Georgetown and I placed her as a recruiting assistant at a large D.C.-based law firm. Ally reached out to me when she had questions about her role and how she could be most valuable to her department, and I advised her on ways she could ask her manager for additional responsibilities. Ally came back to me when she was ready for her next role and I placed her in her next position as a coordinator. Ally has stayed in touch with me over the past 13 years. She's asked to meet me for coffee, she's sent me her wedding photos, and she's made sure I know what's happening in her career. I will always take her calls and make time to meet with her because she has stayed in touch and let me know how my advice plays out for her.

Recently, Ally shared with me that she wasn't happy with her latest career move. She had consulted me before she accepted the role and I'd mentioned that her would-be boss had a reputation for being difficult. After much discussion, she decided the bigger title and compensation were worth the risk — but the job turned out to be even more challenging than she expected. I was happy to be there for Ally to support her and even suggested another role that may be a much better fit culturally for her. I would do anything to help her because she has invested in our relationship and shown deep respect. Things sometimes do not work out as you hoped, but if you have a collection of career advisors looking out for you, you are very likely to land on your feet!

I love working with young professionals and making time to advise them on their careers. It's extremely rewarding to witness a young person develop professionally. We more senior professionals want to see you succeed, and hearing from you as you progress on your journey is thrilling!

While Ally is an example of a great mentee, I've also had some not-so-great experiences.

Let's talk about what *not* to do as a mentee.

Over the past 25 years, we've had more than 50 interns work at my company, Wisnik Career Enterprises, Inc. I'm still in touch with many of them. They call periodically to ask what they should do to get promoted or whether they should explore new job opportunities. I welcome these calls! However, there are also a few former interns whose calls I don't welcome — because the only time they reach out is when they need something. Otherwise ... silence.

Have you ever had a friend who only reached out when they were having relationship problems? They'd call or FaceTime or text you novels about their drama, and you'd listen attentively and give them your best advice, and then they'd drop off the face of the earth? Not only did they hardly ever ask about your life, but they wouldn't even update you on their situation. In fact, you wouldn't hear from them for months, until they popped up again wanting advice. I'm willing to bet it wasn't your most fulfilling friendship.

This is similar to what happened with Jane. She worked for us for almost two years while she was attending college in Manhattan. She applied to law school during her senior year and asked me to write one of her letters of recommendation, which I happily did. After she received a few acceptances, she asked my advice on which school to attend: the more prestigious one or the one that gave her more money? After much discussion, she decided to take the money so she wouldn't accumulate even more student debt.

Jane was a very hard worker and did really well in her first year of law school. When it came to on-campus recruiting, because of her stellar academics she was granted interviews with a dozen of the best law firms in New York City. But one morning, she called me in tears. Jane said her interviews were not going well because the partners she was meeting with were doing most of the talking and she didn't feel she was presenting herself well to them. Her Law Review classmates who did the same number of initial interviews were already getting call-backs while she was getting rejections. I stopped everything I was doing to coach her. I encouraged her to take charge of the interview and to provide specific examples of how she performed that would impress and inspire the confidence of these hard-to-win-over partners. Jane ended up with three call-backs, including one with her dream firm. She received one offer for a summer position and was put on hold at her dream firm. I knew the head of recruiting at that firm and took it upon myself to call her and say that Jane was a very hard worker and performed better than she interviewed. If she was on the cusp, I encouraged them to give her a chance. After she received the offer from her dream firm, I told her I'd made the call.

That summer I was meeting with the head of that firm's HR department regarding a few open positions they wanted us to fill. It was halfway through the summer program when I reached out to Jane, letting her know I'd be in her office and asking if we could meet for coffee. After my meeting with HR, I met Jane in the firm's cafeteria and she told me how much she was enjoying her litigation assignments. I didn't hear from Jane when the summer ended and was concerned that she hadn't received an offer to return after graduation. Months later, she finally called because she needed me to verify information from her time working for us for her bar admissions forms. As it turned out, she *was* returning to her dream firm after graduation; she'd just forgotten to tell me.

You may be thinking, "Jane was a busy law student, give her a break!" The important thing to keep in mind is that these relationships go both ways. *Relationship* really is the key word. *If you want a career advisor to be there for you, then you need to take the time to keep them informed.* Tending to the relationship doesn't take much time or effort. I recommend you aim to connect with your career advisors once a quarter and use the holidays as opportunities for re-connection.

Ways To Stay Connected With Your Mentors

Here are some simple, concrete ways to stay in touch and maintain your contacts.

For example, Thanksgiving (my favorite holiday) is perfect for acknowledging people in your life who have been helpful to you. Use the three days before Thanksgiving to send an email or, better yet, call your career advisors to say "How's your year-end going?" or "Thank you again for encouraging me to take X class or being my reference for this role. It's going great!" Make the thanks in Thanksgiving work for you! Sounds silly, but it's much more effective than sending a holiday card in December that gets lost in the pile of mail.

In the winter months, be on the lookout for information such as articles or podcasts that could be of value to your career advisor or something that makes you think of them. Whether you're taking a class or attending a training webinar for work, you'll be learning new things. As you do, ask yourself, "Is this something that could benefit one of my career advisors?" Chances are your career advisor loves being in the know and will appreciate the information.

You can also connect on shared experiences. For example, if you both went to Michigan and you go back on-campus for a football game, buy them a souvenir and drop it in the mail (or, even better, meet them for coffee and give it to them). They will be overjoyed that you thought of them, I promise.

As spring approaches, if you haven't been in touch for a while you can use Passover/Easter or the first day of spring as another marker to reconnect. Ask yourself: "Is there any way I can be helpful to them?" Yes, you can be helpful to your advisors! For example, if their kid just heard back from colleges, you could offer to talk to them about your experience with your fraternity or writing for the school paper. Or maybe they're planning their summer vacation and you have some tips and recommendations to share. The insight here is that even when you're early in your career, you have things to offer more senior people. I recommend ending all conversations with: "Is there anything you're currently dealing with that I can be helpful with?" You'll be surprised by what they may say and how you can be a resource.

September is another great time to solidify your relationship with your career advisors. Many professional associations and alumni organizations ramp up programming as the school year begins. Actively be on the lookout for ways you can make your career advisors look good. For example, if you're head of a business club at school and one of your career advisors is a successful money manager, ask them to be a guest speaker. Your peers will have the chance to learn from this expert and you will shine a light on them. Or if you're writing an article for an industry publication, newsletter or blog, reach out to your career advisor for a quote. You're in charge of how you create and cultivate long-term relationships with career advisors.

Many young professionals think that renowned leaders are off-limits to them. This simply isn't true, so don't shy away from making high-profile professionals your career advisors! For example, last night I had dinner with my daughter Arcadia, who just transferred from a small college in Madrid to Barnard College in New York City. She was exuberant about her new classes, but a bit concerned about the number of students in one of her political science courses. Back in Spain, she'd never had more than 20 students in a class, while this one at Columbia had more than 200. She loved what the professor said in the opening lecture, so she stopped by office hours right away to introduce herself and tell the professor, who's also a renowned civil rights attorney, how excited she was to learn from her.

Now, before you dismiss this as a suck-up move, I want you to consider the professor's reaction. The professor said, "I can't believe you showed up just to tell me how excited you are to learn from me. You just made my day!" She continued to ask Arcadia about her background and shared that she'd also double-majored in Spanish and political science when she attended Barnard in the 1980s. This was a big bonding moment, and all it took was for Arcadia to swing by office hours for a quick chat.

The most successful professionals are motivated by legacy. This means they want to support the success of up-and-coming young professionals like you! They love paying it forward — all you have to do is acknowledge their guidance and stay in touch.

How to Build a Professional Network

The most successful people I know got where they are by fostering lifelong professional relationships. Building a treasure chest of contacts is a major key to creating a successful career, and it's one you have control over. I have witnessed this over and over again. The economy is cyclical, and companies will periodically downsize, but with great professional relationships you'll have a safety net you can fall back on in the most uncertain of times. Invest in your relationships!

Before I dive into the steps you can take to build a professional network, I need to shatter another Big Lie that is rampant and sounds something like: "This is all well and good for people who are well connected, but I'm not one of them. Successful professionals aren't accessible to me." I want to reassure you: You can start building a network now by cultivating key relationships you *already have*. I'll show you how.

When I was at Barnard I noticed that many of my classmates had well-connected parents who could introduce them to colleagues who, in turn, could help them land lucrative summer jobs. This wasn't the case for me: My dad owned a candy store in the Bronx and didn't graduate from high school. I came to the United States as a political refugee when I was 5 years old and had no relatives here other than my immediate family. I had to create a network from scratch, but I did it and so can you!

During college, I became actively involved in leadership roles and clubs I was sincerely interested in. I was elected as a representative to the Barnard Board of Trustees, served as a liaison to our career services office, and worked in admissions (early signs I was meant to be a recruiter, which I ignored when I blindly went for a Wall Street job!).

Attending Board of Trustees meetings was an incredible opportunity to be in a room full of industry leaders and very successful adults from law, financial services, and the arts. I had never had exposure to professionals like these before, and I was intimidated as hell! I remember each meeting started with a cocktail hour for people to chat with each other. I had never attended a networking cocktail event before. If you have, you may know there's a dance that happens where you chit chat with one person for five minutes before you switch places and speak to the next person. At my first meeting, I got so nervous that I missed the switch and found myself standing all by myself in the middle of the room. I ended up downing two glasses of sparkling wine so quickly that my head started spinning and I began slurring my words. I was so mortified that I retreated to the restroom and stayed there until the formal meeting began. I can laugh now, but I was truly terrified at that first meeting!

I learned so much over the next two years of attending those meetings, including not to drink more than one glass of wine at any professional gathering and, even more importantly, to come prepared to ask questions. I started asking the trustees about agenda items, but also about how they built their restaurant empire or what advice would they give to a college junior that they wished someone had given them.

I highly recommend that you put yourself in uncomfortable situations where you have to interact with successful adults. The more you do it, the more comfortable you will get. This can include people already in your life, such as your next-door neighbor who works in finance who has known you since you were 10, or your best friend's mother who runs a non-profit. If like me, you didn't grow up surrounded by educated professionals, reach out to your supervisors and alums for this kind of mentoring. You can start by asking them what they love about their work and what the young people they work with do to help them most. They will appreciate your asking and you will learn from them!

Another way I built my network early on in my legal recruiting career was by getting involved with professional associations to meet peers and industry leaders. I volunteered to be on committees and made a point to meet new contacts at industry events. A number of professionals I met in those early days are my clients today.

I ramped up my networking efforts even more when I launched my business. One thing I did was have breakfast with two contacts each week. I chose breakfast because it was too early to cancel, didn't interfere with business professionals' workdays, and was less expensive than lunch or dinner. I also wrote letters (there was no LinkedIn) directly to business leaders I read about in industry publications or business journals. I told them how much I admired their work and asked if they could meet me for coffee or speak over the phone to answer questions about how they built their successful careers. Eighty percent of the people I reached out to said yes and became part of my network.

I've actually been teaching networking for a couple of decades. When I was building my business, I taught classes on networking at many of the university clubs in New York, including the Penn Club and the Cornell Club, as well as at NYU Stern Business School, bar associations, and charity organizations. At one point in my career, I was an adjunct instructor at The New School and NYU's School of Continuing Education, where I taught this subject because it's the most powerful career tool.

Over the years I've solidified five ground rules for successful networking:

1. You already know or will meet everybody you need to know to have a successful career. When I observe the connections my kids (who are all in their late teens and twenties) harness on social media, I'm envious. I wish I had connected with and could stay in touch with people I met early in my life and career! Some of the kids you went to camp and middle school with will one day be in a position to help you. Connecting now and (most importantly) staying in touch over time is how you begin building a strong business network. Take every genuine opportunity to positively comment on your contacts' posts and meet up with them when you're visiting their school or city. A coffee date is a perfect way to know what's happening in their lives and to stay connected. Make this a habit and start investing in your relationships now!

2. Don't assume only people in powerful positions can help you. Many people are under the illusion that there are certain "right" people they must meet in order to land a great job. This is a myth. Yes, it's helpful if your college roommate's dad is the president of a company you really want to work for and has heard great things about you from his son, but you don't have to know people in high places to successfully launch your career.

3. If you really don't like someone, don't add them to your network! Strong business relationships are based on trust, and if you don't like someone then you won't build that trust with them. Occasionally, I would reach out to someone I read about and they would agree to speak on the phone but were clearly not interested in sharing their experiences; they acted as though our call was a big pain for them. Or I met with someone for breakfast and the stories they shared were self-centered and negative and made me feel that this was not someone I wanted to meet with again. In these rare cases, I concluded that I didn't want them in my network. I recommend you focus on building relationships with professionals who are generous and understand the value of building professional relationships, even with those who are just starting out their careers and accept that this way of thinking is not in everyone's DNA.

4. Stay in touch with your connections when you don't need anything from them. The best networkers, like the best mentees, are always thinking about their contacts and actively on the lookout for resources that might help them. If you see something that reminds you of a person in your network, reach out and share the information, whether it's an invite to an alumni event or an article that could be of interest. It's actually more important to stay in touch with the people you know and like than it is to constantly meet new ones. The best networkers are constantly thinking about how they can help others and taking action to demonstrate that they are!

5. Introduce your network to each other. One of the most powerful things you can do to solidify your relationships is to introduce contacts to each other. When you become the catalyst for new relationships, both people will be grateful to you. This includes playing "matchmaker" for roommates, jobs, and romantic relationships alike. If you know two people who can be helpful to each other because they will be attending the same grad school or moving to the same city, connect them!

The Value of Informational Interviews and How to Conduct Them

Whether you're looking for an internship or your second job out of college, start the search by thinking of everyone you already know who could give you advice, not necessarily a job. If your friend's mom, your neighbor from home, or your uncle works in real estate and that's your target job area, reach out to them and ask if they can answer a few questions. Before you start applying for jobs, you need to learn how the particular industry works, what makes someone successful, and what skills are required. This is valuable information you can learn by setting up informational interviews. They're powerful tools and they result in real job opportunities more frequently than you might imagine.

Here are some specific tips for how to conduct informational interviews:
• **Approach the professional you want to meet with thoughtfully.** If you have a common contact, ask that person for an introduction. If it's someone you've read or heard about, write them a sincere email and outline some great questions you'd like to ask them so they know you won't waste their time.
• **Prepare for the meeting by doing research.** Start with a LinkedIn search and visit their company's website or Google search. Come to the meeting with a list of questions that go beyond "Tell me what your typical day is like." I suggest asking them about their career path and referencing something you learned about them through your research such as, "I noticed you worked for a Big Four accounting firm prior to heading up communications at a law firm. How were the two work environments different?" Asking more

informed questions will allow you to walk away with valuable insights rather than generic responses.

- **Stay in touch!** I hope you've noticed by now how important this one is. Many informational interviews turn into new job interviews or referrals, but it can take time. Every few months, send updates to people you did informational interviews with to let them know where you are in your career. By doing this you will make them your mentors and they will be more likely to think about you when a new role comes along. I see proof of this everywhere I look, including in our own office: One of our current college interns did an informational interview with an in-house recruiter, who then referred her to us!

Action Plan

Develop a list of 10 key contacts and keep it in your phone for easy accessibility. These key contacts can include people who have already been helpful to you (such as professors, professionals who have been career advisors to you, people you've worked for), as well as the types of professionals you want to meet.

For example, if you're targeting PR firms for an internship, identify five top PR firms and add them to your list:

1. Professional who works at Edelman
2. Junior Associate at Ruder Finn

>H>> >H>> >H>>

As you network and conduct informational interviews, even with those outside of PR, ask them: "Do you know anyone who works for a PR firm like Edelman or Ruder Finn?" I bet you'll benefit from the idea of six degrees of separation and someone will say something like, "Actually, yes, my friend's sister just started at a PR firm in Chicago." Then ask them to introduce you. This may feel uncomfortable at first, but most professionals are happy to talk about their new (or newish) roles and even share how they landed them.

Another thing you can do is research LinkedIn for target contacts. Let's say you're interested in consulting firms for your first job out of college. Identity the names of consulting firms in the city you want to live in. Once you come up with five to 10 firm names, run a search in LinkedIn for associates with one to five years of experience at those firms. Then review each person to see if you have anyone in common, and if you do, ask that connection for an introduction. If you don't have anyone in common, read each profile to find something you share in common, such as schools, home states, clubs/organizations, or interests. Again, I am willing to wager that if you review 20 young professionals' profiles, you will find a few where you have a shared contact or experience. Your job is to find this commonality and reach out to ask if you can ask about their work and what advice they'd give to someone who wanted to follow in their footsteps.

I promise this strategic method of proactively identifying professional contacts you want to meet and seek advice from is much more effective than blindly sending tons of resumes to firms. One method looks like a dartboard with multiple clearly identified targets, while the other looks like a blank white wall with an unknown target. Which do you choose?

Yes, while you're starting to build relationships with career advisors and professional contacts you will feel uncomfortable, maybe even vulnerable. But here's an insight and hopefully a motivator: If you don't ask, you don't get! It's normal to feel fear when asking someone for help, whether that's requesting an introduction or emailing someone you don't know. But if you can train yourself to associate that uncomfortable feeling (I feel mine in the pit of my stomach) with new possibilities, you can rewire your brain to form a positive association to opportunity with that feeling, instead of fear or dread. Over time you will even welcome that uncomfortable feeling because it means you're taking charge of your career and getting closer to achieving your goals!

Key Contacts List

Name
_____

Phone
_____

Email
_____

Address
_____

Name
_____

Phone
_____

Email
_____

Address
_____

Name
_____

Phone
_____

Email
_____

Address
_____

Name
_____

Phone
_____

Email
_____

Address
_____

8 INTERVIEWING INSIGHTS AND STRATEGIES

Another rampant Big Lie tells young professionals that they can't land a good job because they don't have enough experience. This is not true. I have placed and hired hundreds of new grads who had limited work experience but were able to present their skills, work style, and willingness to work hard so clearly that they were hired over others who had more experience. Instead of worrying about what you don't have — significant years of work experience — I want you to focus on what you have acquired from your educational experiences, internships, and extracurriculars, and be able to convey these assets enthusiastically in a cohesive narrative.

If you can do this (and I'll show you how), you will stand out. Having interviewed more than 11,000 candidates for competitive roles, I have to report that the majority would get a C in interviewing if it were a class in school. How do you rise above average and shine in a job interview? In this chapter I'll shed light on what employers want to hear from you, how to prepare for your interviews, and how to avoid the biggest mistakes interviewees make.

Not only have I gained my own insights from conducting thousands of interviews, but I've also talked to many people who hire new professionals. Since 1996, I have taught interviewing skills to decision-makers at more than 70 of the best law firms in the United States. I train these interviewers to ask questions that will uncover whether the law students they screen on-campus have the ability to succeed in their firms. To determine these traits for success, I've interviewed hundreds of firm leaders to find out what they're looking for when they hire law students who have little or no work experience. The qualities these demanding law firm partners seek can be easily applied to other professions, such as financial services, consulting, and other competitive fields.

To start, let's consider what employers are looking for when they are hiring. In short, they're looking for team players who think proactively, take initiative, are willing to learn, work hard and deliver results.

I'll expand on these competencies in chapter 10, called "What Bosses Love," but here's a quick summary of what each one means.

- **Team player:** Has a collaborative work style and works well with lots of different styles
- **Thinks proactively:** Thinks ahead and anticipates needs and possible solutions
- **Takes initiative:** A self-starter who has the confidence and judgment to own their assignments
- **Results-focused** Focuses on achieving outcomes and produxing results/solutions/deliverables
- **Willing to learn:** Knows that they don't know; takes feedback well and is invested in learning
- **Works hard:** Is internally motivated to get things done, even grunt work, with enthusiasm

The very fact that you're reading this book tells me you have these qualities. But can you communicate them clearly? *Your goal during the interview process is to show evidence that demonstrates how you developed these traits through your school and work experiences.* Approach your interviews with a strategic plan: Identify what you want your interviewer to know about what you bring to the role you're interviewing for. This proactive approach will allow you to take charge of your messaging and ensure you provide evidence to back up why you're the right candidate for the role!

Your Strategic Plan

I advise you to start with the key traits outlined above and choose three that you believe are critical for the role. Write out two or three vignettes that illustrate how you used or developed this trait. For example, if you want to demonstrate your work ethic, you can share:

Last semester was particularly challenging as I was taking five classes, working 15 hours a week, and writing my senior thesis. What I am particularly proud of is how I was able to manage my time by making a schedule on Sundays that allowed me to allocate time for the thesis. I think learning how to prioritize and juggle multiple important demands will serve me well as I begin my first job out of college.

In addition, I urge you to review the job description for the position you're interviewing for. Choose at least three responsibilities on the job or requirements and find compelling examples from your background that can showcase how you fulfill them. This could include sharing with your interviewer something that sounds like this:

While reviewing your job description, I noticed that you're looking for an intern who has social media experience. I created and managed the Instagram account for my sorority. We actually won the "Best Instagram Chapter" out of 60 chapters that were considered. I think ours stood out because of the consistency of the artwork and how many of our chapter members are active posters. It took some time and effort to get participation, but I learned so much from analyzing the data and figuring out which posts got the best engagement. I would really like to bring this experience to your company.

Your goal for each interview should be to *provide your interviewer with clear examples of the key traits you possess and the experience you have that matches the job description.* By preparing your strategic plan and communicating what you're excited to bring to their workplace, you'll be in a great position to convince them why you're the right hire.

In addition to creating an interview strategy for each position you interview for, you have five more tasks to master: Be prepared to answer the two most frequently asked questions, queue up smart questions to ask of your interviewer, know what *not* to ask, develop a compelling narrative, and follow up after the interview.

Let's start with preparing for the two questions you must be able to answer. These questions always get asked, whether directly or indirectly:

- Why are you interested in the company?
- Why are you interested in this role?

Let's dissect each one to identify what the interviewer wants to hear from you so you know what a good answer sounds like.

Why are you interested in this company? *The interviewer is trying to gauge whether you did your homework and have compelling reasons for wanting them.* Back when I was in college, one of the Barnard Board of Trustees passed my resume onto a recruiter at Goldman Sachs — a huge opportunity! But when he asked me "Why Goldman?" I bombed because all I really knew was that it was a prestigious firm. Not great. You don't want to emulate my naivete!

Here's what a good answer sounds like: "I spoke to one of your interns who attends my college and she told me about your rotational program. This really piqued my interest because I want to spend my summer applying both what I learned in my marketing classes and utilizing the finance concepts I have been studying." This is a strong answer because it demonstrates that you did your homework and showcases that you have skills and knowledge you are excited to bring to this internship.

Why are you interested in this role? *The interviewer wants to know how well you know yourself and what you're excited to bring to this position.* This is why it is so important for you to know yourself and to have a clear understanding of your unique skills, values and workstyle. Remember how I chose banking right out of college, but didn't have the skills or motivation to do analytical number crunching? I shouldn't have gotten past my on-campus interview and landed that role. I don't remember the details of that interview, but if the interviewer had asked this question or paid attention to the answer I'm sure I would not have gotten past my first round of interviews.

It's important that you clearly articulate what you have to contribute to the role you're interviewing for. Remember: Significant work experience is not the only compelling answer! For example, you can say something like: "I would like an opportunity to contribute the strong writing skills that I have been able to fine-tune in my journalism and English classes." Or, "This semester I'm working on a group project where we're writing a marketing plan. It's been a great experience and I am excited to use these skills on your business development team." Or, "In conducting research for my professor, I have used Excel a great deal and would like to use these skills to create pivot tables for the data analysis mentioned in your job description."

To ace your interview, you must prepare and be able to share specific examples that illustrate what you learned from your school projects and other learning experiences that have developed your skill set, and that you can now bring to this role. Knowing your unique talents and having evidence to share with your interviewer is key to landing a great job, even if you don't have direct work experience. You have control over this! (Make sure to review your top skills and values assessment from chapter 2).

Asking Smart Questions
(and Knowing What Not to Ask)

Answering questions in ways that illustrate your skills and capabilities isn't the only way to show you've done your homework on the company and know yourself well. If you want to stand out from the crowd, it's also important to **ask** great questions.

Powerful questions you can ask sound like:

- I noticed on your website that you are expanding into the agricultural industry. How do you think that will impact your overall business strategy?
- Could you tell me a little about how your master's in international relations has helped you in this field when most professionals have an MBA?
- I noticed in the job description that you're looking for candidates who can build relationships across the firm. Can you tell me a little about who this new hire would be working with outside the department?

Don't Ask This!

On the topic of asking questions, be aware that there are types of questions you *shouldn't ask,* too. First, avoid asking self-serving questions aimed at making you look smart. Complex questions loaded with big words can make the interviewer feel dumb, plus they come across as insincere (you really don't care about the answer and probably already know it). I have never seen someone get hired who makes the interviewer feel inferior or comes across as a pompous jerk.

Second, stay away from the types of questions that are all about you and what you want, especially in the early stages of your interview process. At this stage, your goal is to present what you can bring to the role and how you can benefit the company. *Frankly, the interviewer doesn't care about what you want until they want you.*

Don't ask questions that can be easily answered by reading the company's website or marketing materials. (For example, "How long is the training program?" and "Will the company pay for my Series 7/bar exam/etc.?") If you ask these questions, it shows that you didn't do your homework. Also, don't ask questions that are self-focused, e.g. "When could I expect to be promoted?" This question is a definite NO! You haven't even gotten in the door and already you want to know when you'll get promoted? This is a red flag that you're self-interested and may quit as soon as something better-sounding comes along. It makes the interviewer question why they would invest in you.

Creating a Compelling Narrative

In addition to creating an interview strategy that will provide evidence you possess traits and experiences the interviewer is looking for in candidates, you should create a compelling narrative that tells your story. There are two reasons I want you to invest time in writing out your narrative. First, you must be able to respond well when the interviewer says, "Tell me about yourself." And second, I want you to be able to clearly communicate the themes that *you* want your interviewer to know about you, especially if they don't ask good questions to solicit this information (which happens more frequently than you might imagine).

You need to tell your story in a succinct, positive, and engaging way. I recommend practicing by answering the frequently asked "Tell me about yourself" conversation starter. This non-question question is intentionally vague and it's your job to tell the interviewer what they need to know about you that makes you a great fit for their role.

Here are a couple of things to think about as you develop your compelling narrative:

First: Provide specific examples that clearly illustrate what skills and competencies you bring to the role and company. The best interviewees paint a clear picture of what they've learned that will enable them to add value. They don't speak in generalities like: "I had a lot of responsibility at my job last summer." Instead, they say: "Last summer I had to open and close the restaurant when my manager was on vacation for two weeks. This included monitoring inventory and placing orders, tracking our team members' hours for payroll, and closing out each day's earnings. There were so many important details to keep track of daily to run the business that I developed a checklist which my manager still uses today. It was challenging but a great learning experience! I really enjoyed that level of responsibility and I think it prepared me well for this role." I urge you to come up with compelling narratives that are easy to grasp and illustrate the skills and competencies you developed and can bring to the specific role you're interviewing for.

Second: Your story has to provide a strong sense of what motivates you and it needs to convey your ability to get results. For example, if you were the communications head of the pre-law society and published an article while maintaining a full course load, you may want to illustrate how you managed your time and juggled multiple priorities. You could say something like: "It was a hectic semester. I'm proud of the article I wrote that got published and also for successfully promoting our speaker series using the Mailchimp newsletter I launched. I think I was able to achieve these results because I developed a plan where I blocked out time on my schedule between classes and broke these big projects into doable steps. I'm excited to bring my time and project management skills to your company."

As I said above, you want to focus your answer on the specific role you're interviewing for. If you're targeting a few different industries or roles, you should customize your narrative and examples to each one. When I'm preparing candidates for their interviews, I always use the job description as our guideline. We refer to the key responsibilities and develop examples that will show the interviewer that the candidate has the skills to do the job. You should do this too.

Avoid Common Interviewing Mistakes

Now that you know what makes a candidate shine in an interview, let's talk about what mistakes can land you in the rejection pile. Based on feedback I've received from thousands of interviewers, I've identified four common mistakes interviewees make. Let's review them now so you can avoid them in the future. The good news is that these are all things you have control over!

Mistake #1: *They don't prepare well.* The candidate can't articulate why they're interested in the company and what they could bring to the role. Or they ramble and don't answer the questions asked. The solution here is simple: Do your homework!

Mistake #2: *They can't speak to things on their resume.* It should be a given, but I can't emphasize enough how important it is for you to be able to speak to *everything* on your resume, even if it was a job you held one summer a long time ago. It's not okay to say, "Well, that was a while ago, so I don't really remember." It's also a big mistake to exaggerate your responsibilities on your resume and then not be able to discuss them in a specific, articulate way. You don't need to embellish what you did — your job as a server in a restaurant can be fodder to illustrate your customer service skills, hard work, reliability, and problem-solving abilities. Your homework is to identify examples and create a narrative that will showcase your skills and work style.

Mistake #3: *They're nervous and don't inspire confidence.* Interviews can be intimidating, but if you practice speaking about things you did well and are proud of, you will naturally convey enthusiasm and confidence. Even if you're introverted or don't like bragging about your achievements, you can prepare stories to share that illustrate successes you achieved and obstacles you overcame. Have stories ready to tell that will clearly demonstrate the skills and workstyle you can contribute without having to straight-up say, "I'm great at X."

Mistake #4: *They speak negatively about past employers, colleagues, or experiences.* Not all job experiences are good ones, but an interview is *not* the time to bash past employers (or anyone else), because this reflects badly on your judgment and professionalism. Even if your first job out of college was boring and your boss was a micromanager, you don't want to go there when answering the question, "Why are you looking for a new role?'" Instead, you will be much better served by putting a positive spin on things and saying, "I'm glad I had this experience; it further developed my detail orientation and appreciation for proofing my emails extensively. I am now ready for a new challenge where I can bring my strong work ethic and take on more responsibility."

How to Answer Difficult Questions

There are a few commonly asked questions that young professionals dread. Don't freak out — I'm here to show you how to handle tough questions!

Difficult question #1: *"What's your greatest weakness?"* I discourage you from answering with anything that sounds like "I'm a Type A personality" or "I'm a perfectionist." We all know that's a BS answer, and as you read in chapter 3, being a perfectionist is *not* a good thing! What I advise you to do instead is to sincerely share a weakness and then pivot to tell your interviewer how you've worked to improve it and what you're excited for. You can say something honest like, "I don't have direct experience in analyzing financial data, but I did use SPSS to analyze psychology research and I think the summaries I drafted for the professor helped me to fine-tune my writing skills. I'm excited to bring these research, analysis, and communication skills to this role." By sharing a real weakness, like not having direct experience, you will come across as trustworthy — you know what you don't know — and by providing examples that show your potential or how you mastered the unknown, you will inspire confidence that you can learn.

Difficult question #2: *"Where do you see yourself in five years?"* When the interviewer asks this question, what they *really* want to know is whether you're planning to stay in this industry, ideally with this company, in five years. So the only right answer is something like, "I see myself as a fifth-year associate/VP with your company." But you also need to have a good reason why. For example, "I've read about your impressive statistics on tenure and would love to be one of the 70 percent of hires who are with the company five years later." Or, "I know it takes a few years of on-the-job training to learn what clients need and how to solve their problems. I'm looking to build a career, not just for a first job out of college." Or, "Having had the experience I had, I'm looking for a forever home and would really like to stay with my next firm for a long time."

Your interviewer's fear is that they will train and invest in you and you'll leave within several months or a couple of years. I've been in hiring meetings in which the committee concludes, "He's a great candidate, but he won't stay. Let's pass on him." You need to demonstrate during the interview that you will be a good *investment*, not just a good hire.

Difficult question #3: *"Explain your GPA."* Whether your interviewer has reviewed your transcript or not, you have to be ready to address any problematic grades on your record. I've sat in on many hiring decision meetings, and when a candidate's file is being reviewed, we read over the interviewer's evaluations and transcript. If there is an anomalous grade, someone will always ask: "Why did he get a B- in his Intro to Philosophy class?" If there is a clear answer (e.g., someone who interviewed you shared what you said about the professor being new to the school and grading on a C curve), it helps those making the decision. If there is no clarifying information, someone on the committee will make up a story to explain why you got a B- based on *their* experience, not your reality. This may sound like: "I know the type that blows off intro classes because they aren't interesting. The problem is that some of our work isn't that interesting and he'll likely blow that off too. Let's pass on him." This really happens! Now that you know, be prepared with persuasive narratives so others don't make up stories for you.

Follow-ups That Seal the Deal

Once you've aced your interview and left the office/hung up the Zoom call, remember that it's not over! Another way the best candidates stand out is by following up after the interview. Here are a few important do's and don'ts for following up after an interview.

Do send each person you met with a different thank-you note that references your conversation and what you spoke about. Your follow up note is best sent by email because decisions are made quickly and those working remotely will not be in their office to receive a handwritten note. I did once hear a candidate tell me that she wrote the note by hand and then took a photo of the note that she emailed to her interviewer, I thought this had a nice personal touch. Sending a follow-up note is an opportunity for you to distinguish yourself and write about something specific that resonated with you or that you learned from that particular interviewer.

Don't fire off the email from your phone without testing that the fonts and spacing look right. I recommend emailing yourself to make sure the note looks clean. Proofread carefully to confirm that all names are spelled correctly, and remember that many common names have several spelling variations. I've seen candidates lose job offers because the name of the company or interviewer was spelled wrong in their thank you notes. Don't just type "Megan" — make sure it's not Meghan or Meagan before you hit send!

Don't send thank-you notes from your work email or during work hours when you should be working for your current employer.

Do follow up with pieces of work, such as research you've conducted that showcases your analytical skills, school projects that illustrate your writing or creative capabilities, or articles you have published. Providing evidence of the skills you've developed and can bring to the role will make you stand out. But remember: **Don't** share anything you don't own or can't publicly disseminate. For example, if you wrote a piece that's on your current firm's website, then sharing a link with an interviewer is a good move. But sharing internal research you conducted and got paid for is not okay, since that's your employer's property. Doing so will make the interviewer question your ethics and could result in you not getting hired.

Action Steps

Create your compelling narrative! Here's how to do it: Identify three experiences from your resume. They could be leadership roles, classes you excelled in, part-time jobs, research you conducted, or school projects you worked on.

For each experience, write out the skills you developed and are excited to bring to the role you're interviewing for:

1.

2.

3.

Now write a narrative answering the question: "Tell me about yourself." You should include highlights of your academic success, competencies you developed through your experiences, and what motivates you. Make sure to provide details that paint a picture so your interviewer can envision the experiences you can bring to their company.

Here's a great hack that works when preparing for interviews: Write out your full sentence narrative and examples that illustrate what you've learned and can bring to the role. By typing out the words, you'll have easier mental access to them during the interview. You may also want to run your interview narrative past your career advisor to see if it resonates with them and to get their feedback.

9 TIME MANAGEMENT AND GOAL SETTING

Some of you may believe: "I just don't have good time management skills! I wasn't born with them." This is another Big Lie that I want to help you shatter! I've taught time management skills to 8,000 professionals, and I know with total certainty you can learn the skills needed to focus, plan, and execute on the projects and tasks that are most important for you to do. In this chapter, I will share the best time management hacks with you so you have the tools you need to accomplish your career goals as well as deliver timely work products.

Let's start with why developing good time management skills should be one of your top priorities. We all get 168 hours per week, and it's up to us to use them well. In order to make the best decisions with the limited time we get, it's vital to know what we want most— what our primary goals are. So often we just do whatever is vying for our attention, which is to say we're reactive rather than proactive. As a result, we end up feeling like we don't have enough time to do the things that are most important.

The Importance of Goal Setting

Before we get into my time management hacks, we need to lay a foundation. First we'll explore the importance of goal setting, and then we'll look at what it means to invest our time wisely.

I began setting annual goals in 1989 and have found this strategic process of identifying what I want to accomplish each year to be instrumental to my success. I set goals for the number of placements I want to make each year and for special projects, such as launching a podcast. My process includes carving out time the last week of December to both reflect on the past year and plan for the one ahead. You can begin this process any time of the year. I set specific, measurable, and actionable personal and professional goals. This annual goal-setting exercise helps me determine what I want to accomplish and where I want to invest my time and energy in the coming year. Identifying what you want to achieve will help you make the best decisions as to where you spend time for months to come. I encourage you to identify and write down your goals, because knowing what is most important will help you to focus and take advantage of the same 168 hours we each get every week. Remember: *Focus on what you can control!* You have control over investing your time (which is one of your greatest assets), as well as uncovering the things you want to accomplish.

How To Set Goals

Start with identifying a few simple goals in the key areas of your life: career, education, and well-being. Here's an example.

Career: Land a 15-hour-per-week internship where I can use my marketing education
Education: Take 2 courses that expand my writing and analytical skills
Well-being: Exercise 3 times each week for 45 minutes

You can start with just one goal in each category, but you need to make your goals clear and measurable — otherwise, you'll play games with yourself. For example, if you just write down the nonspecific goal that you want to exercise more, then you might end up rationalizing that a 20-minute walk to class meets your goal, even though it doesn't necessarily get you the result you really want.

Once I set a goal, I break it down into actionable steps. I recommend this because a goal like landing an internship or full-time role can be overwhelming! Mapping out steps you need to take and focusing on the process is much more manageable. So let's try this out:

Goal: Land an internship
Action steps: (generate the steps you can think of that would help you secure an internship)

- Make an appointment at my career center on campus
- Update my resume with the marketing project I did for class
- Reach out to my friend's sister who works at Spotify
- Research names of growing companies in the music, arts, and media in the L.A. area
- Research LinkedIn for people who attended my school and now work in marketing in L.A.
- Draft an introduction email I can use to reach out to the contacts I identified, asking for an informational interview

Do you see how breaking down a goal into manageable steps makes it so much more doable? Once you know what you need to do, your next challenge is making the time to take these important actions.

The 80/20 Rule

Before I share specific tools that will help you focus and create time for these important actions, I want to share an insight that I think will be enormously helpful: 80% of your desired results come from 20% of the actions you take. This "80/20 rule" is key to understanding how to invest your time so you'll get the best return on your efforts. For example, on the list of action steps above for landing an internship, reaching out to your friend's sister who works at Spotify is probably a 20% action because it'll most likely get you better results than researching names of companies.

Something I want to make you keenly aware of: *Taking high return actions will probably make you most uncomfortable.* For example, calling someone directly will be most impactful in helping you land that internship, and therefore it's the best use of your time, but it's also most likely uncomfortable. Remember when I told you vulnerability is a superpower? Well, this is when the rubber meets the road! *When you're identifying the actions you need to take in order to accomplish your goals, feeling vulnerable is a good indicator that a particular action will be well worth your time!* The actions that stir up feelings of vulnerability are very likely the 20% actions that net 80% of your results.

Take One Action a Day Towards Your Most Important Goals

It can be helpful to think of time as a currency. You can invest it in actions that have a high return, like networking, or a low return, like mass emails to companies you don't have any connections to. We can easily fool ourselves into thinking we're doing something productive to advance our goals when we take these low return actions... and then we get frustrated when we don't get the results we want. Don't waste your time and set yourself up for disappointment. *Identify the high return actions that will get you closer to your goal and commit to taking one of them every day!* I call this my "one action a day" rule.

Here's how it works: Every day I identify one thing I must do that I know is the best action I can take to advance my most important goals. For example, I call a client who hasn't given us business in six months to check-in, I create a new promotional piece for a virtual interviewing program, or I email a referral who has expertise in digital marketing to ask for his advice on marketing this book. All these actions make me a little uncomfortable (either because they're outside of my comfort zone or require me to stretch my skill set), but my gut tells me they're vital to accomplishing my goals, so I follow through. And remember, I'm committing to just *one* of these actions each day.

Audit Your Time

Before I share the best hacks for managing your time, I want you to get a handle on how you *currently* spend your time. Complete this time management audit:

How do you currently spend your 168 hours a week?

- Work   ____
- School   ____
- Household chores/cooking   ____
- Watching TV   ____
- Internet/phone/video games   ____
- Connecting with family/friends   ____
- Self-care habits   ____
- Worrying about things   ____
- Sleeping   ____
- Exercise/sports   ____
- Other   ____

= 168

If your audit reveals that you're currently not investing

your time well, you're not alone. Many students and professionals "waste" their valuable time playing video games/scrolling social media/binging Netflix and not enough time sleeping or exercising. This exercise is for your self-illumination. *Please take an honest assessment of what's working in terms of where you're investing time well and where you'd like to make some changes.* For example, if you're currently spending zero hours a week on self-care habits and want to spend 20 minutes a day, six days a week meditating or writing in a journal, then your new goal is to spend two hours out of your 168 hours each week on self-care.

Although I firmly believe everyone can master time management skills, being smart doesn't automatically make you good at time management. I've worked with many brilliant students and professionals who have underdeveloped time management skills. While you're in school, this lack of time management skills may not hold you back because as long as you hand in an "A" paper, the professor doesn't care if you stayed up all night to write it. But in the work world, you must have the ability to get stuff done on time, and often you need to show the progression of your work to your boss. But don't freak out if you've always waited until the last minute to do things, because I'm going to share my best time management hacks. These are proven tools that I've taught to thousands of professionals, and they work! If you're motivated to learn these new habits and release your perfectionistic tendencies, you can develop the time management skills to accomplish your biggest goals and be a team member who delivers excellent and timely work products.

5 Hacks for Better Time Management

1. Start each day with an action plan

Identify the three most *important* (not just urgent) things you need to accomplish today. Write down these top priorities where you can easily see them, whether in your planner, on a must-do list on your desk, or in an app on your phone. Knowing what you **must do** will give you the focus and clarity you need to get the most important stuff done, no matter how many interruptions come up. One of these three most important actions should be tied to one of the important goals you set for yourself. *This is where you apply the "one action a day" rule.* For example, even during midterms — when you have to finish the outline for your history paper and do research for your philosophy exam — you still spend 20 minutes submitting a resume to a summer internship that came into your email and is exactly what you are looking to do. Taking this one action, even during a busy midterm week, puts you in control of focusing on and achieving your important goal. *Making it a habit to spend at least 20 minutes of each 24 hour day investing in a high return action will add up to massive momentum towards your goals each month!*

If you're currently working, identify available resources that can help you achieve your daily priorities. Mapping out an action plan should include reaching out to colleagues who may have templates or sample work products you can use as you launch a project, as this will help you be most efficient. *If you only think of these resources once you're deep into your project, you may miss out on resources that could have helped you maximize your time.*

2. Create focus time

Block out time for large or long-term work projects so you get in the habit of taking proactive action on the things that are most important. If you're a full-time student, this could be finding a post-college job. If you're working full-time, this might be finishing a big project that's due at the end of the month. If you're currently working, you probably learned pretty quickly that in today's reactive work environment, it's very common to spend eight or more hours at work and only attend to reactive tasks. *Get in the habit of blocking out one or two 30-minute periods each day to take action on long-term projects, ideally at the beginning of your day when you're least likely to be interrupted.* If you're searching for a job or internship, committing a minimum of 30 minutes each day to identifying opportunities, applying for roles, or conducting informational interviews is realistic and a great investment of your time.

To keep yourself motivated on long-term projects, such as a senior thesis or a big work assignment, it's important to keep track of your progress, as well as your to-do list. Recording the steps you've taken on large, long-term projects will show you the progress you're making and will help you maintain interest and focus to the end.

3. Do the worst things first

Do you tend to put off the more challenging tasks on your to-do list and busy yourself with the easy ones instead? You can go ahead and say yes: Most of us do this at least some of the time. But if you don't want to feel that vague, looming dread all day or scramble at the last minute to complete your top priority, make it your mission to *do the worst things first!*

What this looks like is getting in the habit of taking action on your most challenging priority before 11 a.m., no matter what. Your best clue as to which action is the "worst"? It's the one that makes you feel uncomfortable: the paper you have no idea how to start, the work assignment in an area you're unfamiliar with, the needed phone call with an intimidating person. I recommend breaking these large and overwhelming projects into steps and then taking one action. (If the task is something like a single phone call that you're dreading rather than a longer-term project, step one can be to write a script for yourself.) By doing so, you will begin to weaken the perceived threat and take control. "Waiting until later" to tackle the task may sound appealing at 9 a.m., but it will suck your energy and gnaw at your self-confidence, and you won't be able to show up and be fully engaged in anything that day. *Avoiding what you know you need to do is an energy suck.* The price we pay when we don't take action on our "worst things" is high, so do the worst things first!

4. Stop interrupting yourself

Have you ever found that when you're super busy and

have too much to do, you're especially susceptible to interruptions? The trouble with this is that it often takes longer to refocus on the project or assignment you were working on than it takes to deal with the actual interruption. And do you know who's most likely to interrupt your flow of work? That's right: You are! Self-interruptions are by far our biggest culprits. The good news is that I have a practical tool that will help you focus! It's called a **Parking Lot**. Here's how you use it: When you sit down to work on an important project, make sure to have a piece of paper nearby titled "Parking Lot." This sheet of paper is where you'll write down all those thoughts that pop into your mind and distract you when you're trying to concentrate.

As I sit here writing this chapter, I've had at least six thoughts pop into my head about what else I could, or should, be doing. Some are important things I must do today and some are trivial thoughts. Instead of stopping my creative flow completely, I use my Parking Lot to record what I need to do when I'm finished writing this chapter. I jot down things like "order Hawaiian cookies for clients gifts" and "send interview training flyers to new clients," without stopping to actually do these things. Yes, each one will only take a few minutes, but they're likely to result in further distractions that will break my concentration. *If you can stop interrupting yourself, you too will be able to focus on your priorities!* This takes a lot of practice, but the Parking Lot method helps a lot.

5. Establish a 3 o'clock check-in

You can pick a different time that works for your schedule, but the point is to have a set time each day when you stop what you're doing to evaluate what you've accomplished, reassess your priorities, and determine what you must do before the end of the day. Especially if you're working, priorities can change throughout the day and what was at #3 on your to-do list at 9 a.m. may now be replaced by something that came in at 2:30 p.m..

Setting a check-in time before 5 p.m. to re-evaluate your workday and what you must complete will also give you time to tap into existing resources. For example, consider a busy junior attorney who doesn't check in with himself to re-prioritize and instead figures, "I'll get to that important memo at 5, when the emails stop coming in." Then 5 o'clock hits and he goes to start the memo only to realize the librarian is no longer available to help him with research he needs to complete in order to draft the memo. If he'd checked in at 3, he would've been able to shuffle his tasks and prioritize what was most urgent, leaving other important but less timely tasks till after 5. *By setting a time each day to assess what you must do before your day ends, you will be able to plan and strategize how to use your time best.*

Action Step

Assess on a scale of 1-10 how strong you are at the skills that result in good time management:

- Goal setting
- Planning
- Prioritizing (doing the worst thing first)
- Blocking out focus time
- Organizing (creating systems to manage information/resources)
- Communication/managing expectations
- Using resources (e.g., electronic calendar, project management tools)
- Managing interruptions (especially self-interruptions)

Action Step

What goals do you want to achieve this year? Identify the two time management skills you want to further develop that will help you to achieve these goals.

10 WHAT BOSSES LOVE

In this chapter, I want to share what thousands of managers have told me their top performers do that inspires their confidence and makes them stand out. These insights will help you exceed expectations and be an incredibly valuable asset at work. As you might suspect, the first thing I'm going to do in this chapter is shatter a Big Lie! This particular lie says that graduating from a good school with a solid resume prepares you to be a great contributor. The truth is,what your boss will treasure boils down to your ability to get the right stuff done efficiently and on time. This requires competencies such as thinking proactively, taking initiative, using judgment and working hard.

Results From Surveying Company Leaders

I surveyed C-suite professionals and directors (and conducted one-on-one interviews with dozens of them), and I want to give you specifics as to what traits they love in the young professionals on their teams. After analyzing the data, I boiled these hiring managers' feedback down to 10 critical traits and behaviors that bosses love. *Great news: You have the potential to learn and acquire all of them.* I know how motivated you are to perform well at your dream job and that you're committed to mastering these competencies - all of which will enable you to excel at work and open doors to future opportunities.

Let's demystify what you need to do to be a superstar contributor at work. Here are 10 traits and behaviors that bosses love:

1. Be self-driven. Many students excel at school because of external drivers such as getting into a good college and fear of failure. These "carrot and stick" external motivators can work while you're in school, since you receive a grade after turning in an assignment or taking a test, and therefore can be consistently motivated by the reward of a good grades. But it's different in the workplace because you don't get immediate feedback or instantly see the rewards of work projects. As a junior member of the team, you may be assigned uninteresting but important grunt work, and it'll be up to you to keep yourself motivated. In addition, you may not even get feedback on projects you completed because your boss is busy or only tells you when something is done incorrectly.

For young professionals who are externally driven, working without getting immediate rewards is challenging. I have personally witnessed that those who are dependent on external rewards and validation have difficulty staying motivated to produce excellent work products. *On the other hand, if you're internally driven and measure your success by how much you learn or by how much you want to contribute to the team, you will be internally motivated to do a great job regardless of whether you receive those external "carrots."* I've observed this in my company's best interns, who go beyond their job description to do things like research new tools for us to use to recruit talent and draft procedures memos for the team. When I ask them what motivated them to take the initiative that was not asked of them, they answer, "I saw an opportunity to add value and I just did it." They were motivated internally to do the best job possible and, as their boss, I loved it!

2. Focus on the right information. This looks like asking the right questions when a project is assigned to you and knowing what you don't know. I have seen high school interns who possess this ability and employees with master's degrees who do not. *It's not just about intelligence and motivation; it's about judgment.* For example, as I mentioned in chapter 3, if someone is a perfectionist or has a high need for significance and to feel smart, they may overthink the situation and make it more complicated than it is. This employee is likely to come to their boss with questions that aren't relevant and point out things that have nothing to do with the problem that needs to be solved, just to show off how "smart" they are, not to add value. I know you don't want to be this team member.

3. Execute and get things done efficiently. This is about being driven to deliver desired results on time. People with this skill are efficient at using available resources. *They map out how they will get to the desired outcome and find the best course of action.* They have strong organizational skills, they create useful templates, and they know how to use technology to maximize their efficiency. These young professionals invest their time and skills wisely and do not procrastinate or distract themselves. Bosses appreciate when you tap into existing resources, including your colleagues and existing precedents. They also place a high value on your well-developed time management skills and ability to prioritize.

4. Utilize practical intelligence. The difference between being a good student and being a good employee comes down to knowing how to *apply* your knowledge to solve problems and make decisions. The young professionals who are of the greatest value to their companies are the ones who can extrapolate theories and turn them into productive tools. For example, studying economics in college is great, but knowing how to look at business trends and make recommendations based on your sound analysis is what makes you a valuable asset. Being smart in school does not automatically make you a good problem solver who will achieve the results your boss needs from you. *To be of greatest value, make sure you are focusing on practical problem solving and are results-focused.*

5. Have situational awareness. The best contributors can size up situations and people and then adjust their work style and communications to meet the situation/person where they are. For example, the young professional who recognizes that a different tone is expected when communicating with partners and adjusts his email to reflect this awareness exhibits this judgment. These young professionals can also quickly grasp the nuances of their work environment (what I call the unwritten rules). For example, they know, without being asked, to CC their boss on all emails that go to decision-makers. As simple as this sounds, they know when their boss can be interrupted with questions and when to wait for the right time. *Your ability to "read the room" and use good judgment inspires your boss's trust.* This in turn not only makes you a valuable member of the team but oftentimes results in you getting more responsibility.

6. Possess grit. The young professional who perseveres on challenging assignments and can recover from setbacks truly impresses. For example, one summer my company had a high school intern who had to read three years' worth of our Wisnik's Wisdom blogs and identify the one that would be best suited for a "blog book" we wanted to create for clients. She spent her entire time with us on this one project. I'm sure this sometimes tedious assignment was boring, but she came to work each day with a smile on her face, ready to tackle the next piece, and we ended up with a great end product to share with our clients. Even when working with an outside printing company became difficult, she persevered and focused on the end result: an error-free and professional booklet with our best career tips. Remember, doing well at work is different from doing well in school. In school, if you don't like a class, you know it will be over in a matter of weeks. But your boss will notice if you lack the grit and perseverance required by work projects that last for months and are not interesting. *Showing grit and a commitment to delivering great work, no matter the obstacle, makes you stand out as an exceptional asset to the team.*

7. Take responsibility, especially when things go wrong. This team member takes ownership of their assignments and full responsibility when mistakes happen. I frequently get feedback from hiring managers praising how someone we placed with them volunteers to take on projects and takes initiative from start to finish. Yes, this team player will check to make sure they are on the right track by sharing an outline for the project with their boss, but they have the confidence and ability to get each step done and deliver an excellent end product.

Taking responsibility is equally important when something goes wrong. Managers have also told me that a pet peeve of theirs is when a team member blames others when things go wrong on a project. (For example: Instead of testing out the online video system before an important meeting, they blame IT for a technology failure.) *Be the young professional who is ready to take ownership and solve issues, instead of blaming others.*

8. Manage expectations. The team members who communicate clearly what work they can or cannot handle are the ones who breed confidence. Instead of feeling like you may disappoint your supervisor by not taking on a project, you're much better off managing your boss's expectations from the start and telling them what you're capable of delivering, time-wise or skill-wise. *By being up-front and not missing deadlines or turning in subpar work, you will build credibility.* This comes down to clear communication. For example, it's very frustrating to me when an intern doesn't manage expectations around when they can be at work. I completely understand that interns have times during the semester (like midterms and finals) when they need time off to study or write papers. All they have to do is give us a heads up that allows us to plan our work accordingly - instead of not showing up and leaving us without the resources we were relying on. By managing your supervisor's expectations you will become a trusted member of the team.

9. Give credit and make others look good. The team members who are quick to give credit to other contributors look good! I'm not suggesting that you don't let your boss know where you contributed, too, but it's important to know that giving others credit reflects well on you. For example, at the start of a meeting when you discuss the report you were responsible for producing, you may want to say: "Before we start, I just want to thank Joe for helping me with the graphics." This is what being a team player looks like! *Bosses love collaborative young professionals who know there is no scarcity when it comes to making others look good.*

10. Have (appropriate) self-confidence. These young professionals have self-awareness and know their strengths and weaknesses. They believe in their ability to accomplish goals and have the courage to take on projects in areas that are new to them. *Yet, they don't project certainty in areas where they're not skilled or knowledgeable.* They know what they don't know. Let me illustrate where the line is between being confident versus losing credibility with those you work for: Law firm partners have frequently reported to me that they lose confidence in summer associates who give wrong answers off the top of their head. The partner always would prefer that the summer associate responds, "Let me look into that. I will get back to you shortly," and then come back with the right answer after doing the research. Having confidence is great. Having misplaced confidence can cause a major career mishap.

Now that you know what you need to focus on and do in order to excel at work, let's go over what *not* to do. There are five big (and common) mistakes young professionals make in the workplace. Keep reading to learn what they are and how to avoid them.

Here are the five biggest mistakes young professionals make:

1. They don't pay attention to the unwritten rules of the workplace. Every workplace has a unique culture that includes "rules" for how things are done. For well-integrated team members these rules are clear, but if you're just entering the department they may be invisible. Naturally, not knowing the unwritten rules means it's easy for you to fumble and make errors.

To illustrate the concept of unwritten rules, think about this: Your family has certain established ways for how things are done, such as how you eat dinner. In our family, we all participate in making dinner and cleaning up, but whoever cooks doesn't have to clean up. When our youngest son lived with a host family in France, his host mother got upset when he tried to help. She saw it as her role to make dinner for the family. Neither way is right or wrong, but you can see how families have their own unwritten rules and if you violate their established way of doing things, you'll look like an outsider.

So how can you avoid violating rules you don't know exist? When you start a new job, pay close attention to how people interact and communicate. The mistakes I have observed young professionals make include not knowing their place and making suggestions or producing work that clearly shows they don't understand the work dynamics or requirements. For example, I've seen interns at my company, in a desire to prove themselves, make suggestions for how we should handle a client situation — but because they don't understand our working history with the client and what this client responds to, their suggestions are wrong and they lose credibility. This may sound harsh, but it's how things go in the workplace. *When you begin a new job, I highly recommend you listen more than you speak and search for a career advisor who can help you to understand the unwritten rules.*

2. They don't project professional presence. My company conducted a study with firm decision-makers on what professional presence looks like. They highlighted five traits:

- Physical presence, which included appropriate attire, poise, good posture, and eye contact
- Interpersonal skills, which included exuding a positive attitude, exercising discretion, and being diplomatic
- Work style: being fully engaged in the work and calm under pressure
- Verbal/communication skills that involved being concise, speaking properly (limited use of "likes" and "ums"), and having a confident voice
- Possessing the personality traits of humility, maturity, thoughtfulness, and a sense of humor

3. They show their unhappiness when they have to do grunt work. As an intern or most junior person on the team, it's very likely you'll be asked to do work that is boring and repetitive. Though it's sometimes maddening, this grunt work may be necessary for a project to be completed and you need to take it on with enthusiasm. Your boss notices when you roll your eyes or put off doing those weekly reports. *By showing an eagerness to help with tedious assignments, you will demonstrate your team-player attitude and inspire your boss's confidence.*

4. They aren't responsive. One of the biggest gripes I hear from bosses is that their junior team members don't respond to emails. I was puzzled at first (were people really blowing off their bosses' emails?!), but then I investigated further. Many young professionals told me they prefer to respond to the email once they have an answer to the question asked or once they've completed the assignment their boss emailed about. This is the exact wrong approach. You absolutely need to respond when you receive the email and say, "I'm on it!" or "I will look into this and get back to you by this afternoon." Your boss needs an immediate response, not necessarily an *answer. Acknowledge that you've received their email, and then email another time once you do have the answer or the completed assignment.*

5. They don't work collaboratively. Knowing how and when to work with others requires a different mindset from the one you needed to succeed in school. In school, you could get an "A" without knowing how to work well with others, but in most workplaces that simply isn't an option. Your boss wants you to collaborate with others — not just those who are part of your team, but people across different departments in the company as well. *By tapping into these resources and showing an ability to build relationships at all levels of the organization, you'll be able to do your job more efficiently and demonstrate your collaborative work style.*

Action Steps

Now that you know what your bosses will love, take a moment to do an honest self-assessment.

Review each of the 10 traits and behaviors that bosses love and honestly rank yourself on a scale of 1 to 10, with 10 being the best:

_____ Self-driven

_____ Focus on the right information

_____ Execute and get things done efficiently

_____ Utilize practical intelligence

_____ Have situational awareness

_____ Possess grit

_____ Take responsibility, especially when things go wrong

_____ Manage expectations

_____ Give credit and make others look good

_____ Have (appropriate) self-confidence

Once you've ranked yourself, identify the top 3 traits you know you have and the 3 you want to develop further.

11 TIPS FOR MANAGING YOUR WELL-BEING

So far in this book, I've focused on sharing insights and information you can use to achieve your goals and be successful in your career. But I've met so many young professionals who didn't make their personal well-being a priority while achieving their professional goals, and they ended up burnt out or developing self-destructive habits. *Well-being isn't some afterthought or nice bonus — it's essential to your success in life and work.* I've also spoken to many young professionals who don't know how they'll find some kind of balance when they're working hard at their dream jobs. In this chapter, I'm going to show you how you can develop healthy habits for maintaining your well-being and for releasing stress. Developing these habits is vital to your long-term success and happiness.

Prioritize Your Well-Being

One of the Big Lies preaches that one day once you've "made it," you will finally make time for your well-being. Unfortunately, I have watched too many high achievers burn out by the time they "make it." It's important that you prioritize your well-being and develop daily practices now that will sustain you throughout your success-filled career. I'll begin by sharing a practical framework you can use, starting today, that will enable you to achieve the work-life balance you seek. Then I'll teach you techniques you can incorporate into your day to care for yourself. My hope is that you will make taking care of your well-being a daily habit.

Let me start with some data that woke me up to how much young professionals are suffering and propelled me to develop a series of well-being programs. In 2016, the American Bar Association released findings from a landmark study in which 32 percent of attorneys under 30 reported having problematic drinking and 21 percent of all respondents reported experiencing high levels of anxiety. Having closely observed how much pressure ambitious young professionals feel, I can understand why addiction and anxiety rates are so high. For example, when I speak to high achievers, they tell me that drinking is an instant statechanger after a long day. It's easy to see how these destructive habits lead to addiction.

I want to share the story of one very impressive professional I met in 1997. I knew her for almost 20 years before I learned about the addictions she'd struggled with that entire time. Being an "A" student her entire life prepared her well to hide her alcoholism and cocaine use and still show up to her law firm jobs and perform exceptionally well.

An Interview with Lisa Smith

Her name is Lisa Smith, and she's the author of the memoir *Girl Walks Out of a Bar*. I have shared her book with many young people, including my own children. Lisa provides real insight into how her perfectionist personality and stress level drove her to drink excessively and become addicted to cocaine and hide both addictions successfully from others. A few summers ago, I invited Lisa to share her journey with a group of my company's clients who are working hard to help change the culture of their law firms and break the stigma of drug and alcohol addiction. Before we go any further, I want to share a Q&A I did with Lisa about mental health and addiction in the legal profession. It's relevant regardless of your own field.

Eva Wisnik (E.W.): What is it about the "lawyer personality" that makes addiction so prevalent?
Lisa Smith (L.S.): It's a great question. Lawyers tend to be bright, hard-working perfectionists. Those qualities, of course, help us get into the profession and succeed in the first place. But that perfectionism can work against us. For many, that begins the day we walk into law school, where substance use and mental health disorders often begin to occur. It's there that we compete against our friends and classmates for grades, spots on the law review, and eventually for jobs. Then there's the nature of the actual practice of law. It's inherently adversarial and we are constantly striving to "win." The demands are heavy, the expectations are high, and thanks to technology, we're never truly disconnected. All those factors together can really impact a lawyer, particularly one like me with a genetic predisposition toward addiction and an underlying mental health disorder (depression, in my case).

E.W.: How has the stigma of mental illness and addiction evolved in the 25+ years you have worked in law firms?
L.S.: That's the good news! We are at a real inflection point in smashing the stigma around these issues. When I first started out, no one ever spoke of mental health disorders such as depression or anxiety. Now we have a whole generation of younger lawyers who grew up understanding that mental health challenges are nothing to be ashamed of and need to be addressed. And the more senior lawyers almost all know someone among their family or friends who deals with such a disorder. It's not a foreign language anymore. Combine that with the tremendous action that organizations like the ABA and Law.com are taking to bring the problem of stigma to the forefront, as well as more lawyers active in the profession speaking publicly about

their own experiences, and you can see real change being made. But there is still a lot of work left to do and a lot of education that needs to take place.

E.W.: Over the past few years, many law firms have signed on to an ABA pledge committing to offering programs that will support their attorneys' mental and emotional well-being. Tell us your thoughts about the ABA pledge and how it could impact how law firms deal with addition in their workplace.
L.S.: The ABA Pledge to Advance Attorney Well-Being is an incredible step forward. In 2016, the landmark study the ABA conducted together with Hazelden Betty Ford found the prevalence of substance use and mental health disorders in the profession to be more than twice that of the general population. Following that finding, the ABA really took action. All of it is premised around the fact that to be a good lawyer, you have to be a healthy lawyer, and that means both physical health and mental health. By issuing the challenge to legal employers to take the pledge, which sets out a seven-point framework for firms to take action, they have given firms and other legal employers (some law schools have signed on as well!) a fantastic roadmap and tools to improve attorney and staff well-being overall.

→»→»→»

Of course, law isn't the only field that reports that its professionals are struggling with mental health and addiction challenges. I recently spoke to a close friend who is an MD and senior leader at a top medical school; she confirmed that doctors are also struggling with mental well-being and addiction. And you may recall my tales from chapter 2 about the excessive drinking and cocaine use I witnessed during my stint at Lehman Brothers. *Why are so many successful professionals prone to mental health and addiction challenges?* There isn't a simple answer when it comes to this question, but from what I've observed, I believe one factor is the enormous pressure they feel to be perfect and to constantly perform at a very high level.

Bottom line: Many high performers don't treat themselves very well, and over time this can lead to destructive habits to get a "break" from all the stress they experience. I'm committed to making you aware early in your career of the traps others have fallen into so you can avoid them. Even if addiction to drugs or alcohol is a non-issue for you, we're all susceptible to different forms of addiction and unhealthy habits that wreak havoc on our well-being: unhealthy diets, long-term lack of sleep, neglecting health issues, chronic stress, and so on. *That's why making it a top priority to take care of yourself is so important!*

If you want to change your stress state after many hours of intense work, you can create habits and rituals that will help you to relax, refuel your depleted "tanks" and nurture yourself. *By making self-care a habit, you will have the energy and mindset to support your achievements.*

Below are the best practices I teach to professionals to help them manage their well-being. I'm very hopeful that if you begin incorporating some of these habits and rituals into your life, you will be able to maintain your mental well-being and feed yourself the primary foods you need to achieve the life you desire.

Focus on Primary Food

Primary Food is a fundamental construct I learned during my year-long training at the Institute for Integrative Nutrition. IIN is the world's largest health coaching school. The curriculum I completed taught me tons of tools to help others achieve their well-being goals through behavioral and lifestyle adjustments. My favorite of these tools is the Primary Food framework, which can help you when you feel out of balance.

Our "Primary Foods" are:
1. Relationships (romantic partners, friends, coworkers)
2. Work/School

3. Spirituality/our connection to something bigger than ourselves
4. Exercise/Movement

When we feed ourselves enough of each of the primary foods, we don't rely on our secondary food (what we put in our mouth; food or alcohol) to fill ourselves up. When you feel out of balance and want to reach for that bag of chips, cookies, or cocktail, you can now use this checklist to self-assess and determine what you *really* need to feed yourself. For example, if you have been studying or working a ton and feel out of balance, maybe you need to schedule a time to hang out with friends (relationships) or hit the gym (exercise). It may be easier to sit on your couch and binge Netflix with your favorite bottle of wine or craft beer, but it's unlikely this will replenish you in the way you need. *Checking in with the Primary Food framework can help you identify what you really need, so you can take control and choose to "feed" yourself what you need to attain the balance you crave.*

You don't have to wait until you feel out of balance in order to do something good for yourself. In fact, in order to function at the high standards you set for yourself, you have to make time to regularly fill your tank. In order to show up in the way we want to for school, work, friends, etc., we *must* make time to engage in activities that refuel us. Self-care doesn't require expensive spa treatments. For example, I find myself recharged by spending time in nature. Before a long day at my desk, I make it a priority to walk in the woods or by the Hudson River because I know it will fuel my productivity and positivity.

Taking care of yourself doesn't have to be complicated. Just take a moment each day to ask yourself: "What will I do to fill my tank and show care for myself today?" It might be exercising, eating a really healthy meal, or getting a good night's sleep. Remember, self-care isn't an "extra" reserved for when you have the time; it's a must if you want the fuel to sustain a long, successful career.

Three Practical Methods to De-Stress:

Clear Your Brain

I suggest starting your day by doing a brain-clearing exercise, especially when you have a lot to do or you're embarking on a new venture, like looking for or starting a new job. When we're overwhelmed with tasks or are going through a transitional time, our fear mind will come up with lots of obstacles, both real and imagined. Even on "normal" days, we all have a monkey brain eager to take over and stress us out. How many times have you really wanted and needed to concentrate on completing a school project and your monkey brain went wild with distracting thoughts? It'll throw everything your way: *What food should I order three hours from now? I need to do laundry. I haven't checked Instagram in a while. I still don't have a job lined up for after graduation.* This brain-clearing technique really helps. You'll need a blank sheet of paper or the notes section of your phone, so sit down and get one of those ready.

Now write down everything that comes into your mind. Don't filter your thoughts. Don't worry if the sentences are run-ons or words are misspelled. It doesn't matter if one thought has nothing to do with the one that came before it. Nothing is too trivial or too serious to write down. Write down all your thoughts. Just get them all out. *By clearing your brain of all these random and distracting thoughts, you will allow space for clear thinking.*

When I started my business in 1996, I used this technique every morning before I went to work. I would write things like: *I don't know if I made the right decision quitting my well-paid job to start this company, I am afraid that I won't have enough clients to sustain my new business, and I'm not sure what to have for lunch today.* My brain excelled at voicing fears and other random thoughts. By purging it of all these thoughts and fears, I was able to start work with a clear mind and really focus on what was most important for me to do that day. If you find your monkey mind running you and preventing you from focusing on what you need to do, use this brain clearing technique to be present in your life.

Focus On What You Can Control

Although there are things in our lives that we can't control, every day we have the choice to focus on the things we can control. The most important one is how we manage our state of mind. For example, you have a choice as to how you react to other people's negativity or fears. It's possible to be an empathetic listener and still guard yourself against absorbing others' negativity. Let's say you have a family member who is very worried about you not having a job after graduation and they project their fear during every phone conversation. When you hang up the phone with them take a moment to say to yourself: *"Their energy is not my energy."* Negative energy is contagious and it is so easy to get enmeshed in others' fears, especially when it comes to those who are close to you. *By taking a moment to consciously distinguish between their emotions and fears from your own, you take back control and responsibility for your state of mind.* This is definitely hard to do, but it is something you have control over.

Express Gratitude

The reason expressing gratitude is such a powerful tool is because fear and gratitude can't coexist. For me, gratitude is the only emotion that is more powerful than fear. Whenever you feel fear or negativity come on (and we're all susceptible to these emotions), or when uncertainty is prevalent, expressing gratitude will dispel these negative emotions.

For example, I make it a habit to send texts or notes expressing gratitude to others who help make my life work. What's amazing is how good I feel when I write the note acknowledging how their action or presence enriches my life. This takes just a minute, but the reward can be immense both for you and the person you're thanking.

Make a conscious effort to really notice the good things that happen every day. I'll share a corny practice that works really well for me: Every time I'm driving and a light turns green just as I approach the intersection, I say "Miracle! Thank you, universe!" As ridiculous as this may sound, acknowledging that something went right and being grateful instantly puts me in a good state. Our mind naturally defaults to seeing what is not working (in the driving example, think road construction, slow drivers, inconvenient red lights, and so on). But just by recognizing what goes right, even if it's something as seemingly silly as a fortuitous green light, we can override this default and begin to train our minds to see all the good things that happen daily. I encourage you to recognize and be grateful for things that go right in your life, such as getting a positive response from a prospective employer or networking contact. *Recognizing and expressing gratitude will help you to proactively manage your mental well-being.*

Establish a Morning Routine

Set yourself up for a productive day by establishing a morning practice. It might include exercising or stretching, spending five minutes meditating with an app, and/or identifying and committing to working on key projects or tasks you want to accomplish. During turbulent times, I don't recommend starting off your day with watching TV, reading headlines, or scrolling through social media. Be wise about how you take in information and how it affects you. You may even want to delete an app off of your phone that triggers you when you read it. Think of information like types of food; some are good for you and some can make you ill. Be wise about how you take in information and how it affects you. You have a choice when it comes to how and when you consume information. Choose wisely.

My morning ritual includes setting intentions by asking myself:

- What do I want to feel today?
- What will make this a good day for me?

Setting intentions helps us to direct our minds and to fuel our action steps. It's like setting a destination for our drive, rather than letting the car decide where it will take you. Our mind needs to be managed, and setting morning intentions is a great way to make sure you're starting off in the right direction.

Create an End-of-Day Routine

After a full day of work or school, your mind is full and you need to clear it and quiet it down. Even at the end of really great days, when I feel good about what I accomplished, I still need to empty some of the thoughts and take stock of all that went well. I equate this end-of-day process to defragging a computer, which is needed so it can function smoothly.

Here are two tips for transitioning from a productive day to a relaxing evening and good night's sleep:

1. The sponge technique. On my train ride home from work, I take an imaginary sponge and I wipe out all the "bad" things that happened that day, including any frustrating conversations or disappointing news. Otherwise, my trouble-finder mind will glamp on to these "bad" things and blow them up and make me feel like it was all horrible. After I wipe out all the gunk, I throw it out the train window. (Don't worry, my imaginary sponge is instantly biodegradable.). I find the sponge technique even helps me to rest after a great day when I am overwhelmed with *good* things that happened. It sounds counterintuitive, but even great news like a promotion or being elected president of a club can be stressful and needs defragging.

2. Another effective end-of-day routine that can help soothe your problem-finding mind is to recall two things that went well that day. For example, if you had a great Zoom interview or finally finished that long-term project that's been on the back burner for months, it can go on your list. Keeping a list of all the things that went right and that we're grateful for gives us some much-needed perspective and sets us up for a peaceful sleep.

Action Steps

Now that you know these techniques for taking care of yourself on a daily basis, identify 2 steps you will take to show more care for your well-being.

For example:
- Which of the Primary Foods do you need more of: work, relationships, movement, spirituality?
- What kind of routine or ritual could you add to the start or end of your day?
- What kind of gratitude practice can you add more of into your daily life?

My Well-Being Action Steps:

1.

2.

12 THE SECRET TO LIVING IS GIVING

In this book, I've shared a lot of information and tools to help you to achieve professional success. But career success without fulfillment is a real possibility. We already shattered the Big Lie that money and status will make you happy, so now it's time to ask the question: *What do you need to lead a life that's both successful and fulfilling?*

Success Does Not Equal Fulfillment

Achieving a big title, high pay, and corner office without a sense of personal fulfillment feels empty. I've seen too many achievers who finally "made it" only to become depressed. It's like hiking to the top of a mountain only to discover the view isn't all that great. I experienced some of this myself: After 20 years of running a very successful business, one day I woke up and wanted more. At that time, I had vague pictures in my mind of what "more" looked like (a larger enterprise that generated even more money). I didn't yet have a clue that success was an inner game and that real fulfillment came from work that helped make others' lives better. *We all have a human need for contribution beyond ourselves.* This is why the secret to living is giving. It's not just a nice little rhyming I — it's the key to a fulfilled life!

To celebrate my 20th year in business, I joined Tony Robbins's Platinum Partnership. I embarked on this year-long journey because I wanted to surround myself with 300 other successful professionals, 90 percent of whom owned their own business and made more than $1 million annually. Frankly, my goal in joining the membership was to grow my business and make more money. My cohort came from around the world and I was excited to both learn business secrets from them and to be inspired by them.

Throughout 2017, I spent 260 hours studying with Tony Robbins and traveling as far as New Zealand to learn more about business, relationships, leadership, and investment strategies. *I joined to learn how to be even more successful, but what I finally learned was how to feel fulfilled.*

Contributing Beyond Yourself is the Key to Fulfillment

I saved the most impactful program for the end of the year: Date with Destiny (you can get a glimpse into it by watching the Netflix documentary *I Am Not Your Guru*). This program asks you to question your limiting beliefs and create the blueprint for a life that will be both success-filled and fulfilling. When I had to write down my life's purpose, I wrote that I was here to share my learnings with others and to inspire them to lead their best lives. That was probably the moment this book was born. During the course of the five-day event, I had to confront my limiting beliefs and fears. This included releasing my fears around depending on others, feeling vulnerable, and being imperfect.

Achieving success by being driven by competition, scarcity, and fear of failure will never feel fulfilling. Working hard because your perfectionistic voice tells you that you won't be good enough otherwise will not lead to a fulfilling life. I had to struggle through my twenties to find work I'm still passionate about, and in my thirties, I found the courage to start a business I still find challenging. But it wasn't until I was in my fifties that I figured out how to feel truly fulfilled.

I don't want you to wait until you're in your forties or fifties to learn the real secrets to a successful and fulfilling life. My goal throughout this book is to shatter the Big Lies we grow up believing and to help you uncover the truths that will enable you to live your best life. One of those Big Lies says you need to focus on yourself in order to achieve greatness. *But the truth is that when you focus on contributing your unique talents and gifts, both at work and beyond, you'll achieve both success and fulfillment.*

I had glimpses of this truth early in my life. The summer between graduating from Bronx Science and starting at Barnard, I worked in the emergency room at a Bronx hospital (I was planning to be pre-med in college, to meet my father's dream for me, and I figured the volunteer role was good for my resume). My shift was 7 a.m. to 1 p.m. on Saturdays. The emergency room was very busy after lots of Friday night happenings in the Bronx during the peak of the crack epidemic — ambulances frequently rolled up carrying patients who had been shot and stabbed. My job as an 18-year-old volunteer was to let family members know if their loved ones were going to the intensive care unit or the operating room. These were life-or-death situations, and I took them very seriously. My five-hour shifts flew by, and then most Saturday nights I'd go to discos like Limelight and Palladium with my friends (this was back when the drinking age was 18). While I had lots of fun with my friends that summer, when I reflect on that time, what I remember most clearly is how filled with gratitude and fully present I was. I realize now that my morning experience of focusing on others and being of service gave me so much perspective and helped me fully appreciate my life. While I recognized my sense of fulfillment at the time, it took me many more years to fully register that the secret to living is giving. I worked so hard to be successful and was so single-minded in my pursuit that fulfillment was an afterthought.

You Already Have Something to Contribute

I'm always grateful to see young people learn this truth early in life, like when my daughter did community service for her bat mitzvah project. Arcadia was 12 when she started volunteering at SPARC on Friday nights. The program she was part of provided recreational opportunities for developmentally disabled adults. Every Friday night there was a theme, such as a sports night during Big 10 games. Arcadia worked with the professionals in charge to plan events, and she helped participants in a variety of activities, from painting to throwing balls and enjoying snacks. She was always elated when she returned home from volunteering. It was very clear how much she benefited from giving to others, and Arcadia continued to volunteer for the organization long after she fulfilled her service requirements.

Was there a time in your life when you volunteered to help others? For example, maybe you tutored a student who needed your expertise or worked at a soup kitchen or animal rescue. Reflect on this experience: How did you feel afterward? Did the time you spent being of service fuel you to be even more productive when it came to your other responsibilities? Did you feel more grateful for your own life? *In what ways did you benefit from helping others?*

Don't believe the Big Lie that you don't have enough to contribute because you're young. And definitely don't believe the one that says you just don't have the time to help. If you review how you currently spend your 168 hours each week, you are likely to find that you do have 2-4 hours each week to dedicate to helping others! We desperately need your generation to help fix our broken world. As I write these words, we're deep into a deadly pandemic, the former president of the United States insisted that the election was rigged, and our environment is under severe threat. I am truly sorry that we have messed up your world so much! But I have deep faith that your generation will begin fixing it. *Please don't wait until you're successful to contribute your unique talents and help make others' lives better.*

Make Time to Serve Others

While we're shattering Big Lies left and right, let's take on the one that says you have to choose between financial success and a fulfilling, service-oriented life. These two things actually go hand-in-hand. If you follow the guidance I've given you in this book, you can find your dream job, develop a network of trusted contacts who will be there for you when you need them (and when you don't), be of enormous value to your bosses and clients, and achieve your financial goals. *You can also lead a fulfilling life if you make it a priority to contribute your time and talents to help others who need it.* The key is to choose a cause that really speaks to you, one that you feel motivated and excited to help with.

If you haven't yet found a cause you're passionate about, keep trying. It could take a few tries before you find both a cause you care about and people you want to work closely with. But when you do find both, magic happens! I've been in many rooms where the participants were committed to a mutual cause and put their egos and agendas aside. Not only were they able to achieve a ton, but they also felt bonded to one another because they shared and amplified the human need for contribution and community. *The trusted relationships formed when you are working toward a common good will be like gold nuggets in your treasure chest.*

If you're looking for your dream job right now, don't wait to volunteer and help others. *Using your time and talents to be of service will fuel your job search.* You'll be energized by giving to others, you'll know your value, and you'll be able to easily convey it to interviewers. As a bonus, focusing on others will take your focus off yourself and put your life in perspective. Not to mention that the skills you develop as a volunteer are real and useful.

Speaking as an interviewer: If you share with me that you've been volunteering for a political organization and drafting press documents or planning Zoom events, I'll be impressed that you have these skills to bring to my role. If you're soliciting donations for a food bank or organizing volunteers for beach clean-ups, I will be impressed with the skills you're further developing and can bring to my organization.

If you're currently working hard at your first job out of school, you may think, "I don't have time to volunteer and don't even know where to begin." First, do a little research to see if your company sponsors any causes. Human resources should be able to tell you if they work with, say, a local school where you can tutor students or help them with their college applications. Or you can check out the LinkedIn for company bios of some of the firm leaders to see if they sit on boards of charities and nonprofits. Chances are a few of them do, and you can approach them to ask if there's a contact at the organization you can reach out to for volunteer opportunities. Whether you know this firm leader or not, they will remember you for this!

AFTERWORD

You've made it through! I hope that the career tools and mindset you take away from this book help you on your path to achieving all the success you so deserve. Please commit to confronting your inner critic and fear-generating trouble-finder mind that will show up! All successful people are victims of fearing failure and vulnerability; they have just learned to overcome these Big Lies, and you can too. As you put yourself out there, I want you to focus on what you can control and on what you *already* have to contribute to the right employers and bosses. We are all a work-in-progress, and I encourage you to remind yourself that the goal is progress, not perfection. Please replace "failure" with "learning opportunity" in your vocabulary, and always remember — you either learn or you succeed.

As Your Fairy Job Mentor, I encourage you to come back to this book whenever you find yourself facing new career challenges and need information as well as inspiration. As you grow and evolve you will encounter setbacks, and the wisdom within these chapters will be there to guide you forward on your journey. Remember to listen to your gut and don't be afraid of taking smart risks!

Good luck,
Your Fairy Job Mentor

ACKNOWLEDGEMENTS

I wrote this book for the next generation of young professionals and am deeply grateful to my Board of Advisors who told me what content they needed and gave me feedback on all aspects of the book, including the cover design.

Thank you to Christine Aguirre, Sophia Danziger, Natalie Eriksen, Jerry Gregory, Ameerah Jaffer, Sandy Jiang, Samuel Kim, Jacob Lewin, Benjamin Milan-Polisar, Katerina Settle, Alana Tang, and Grace Weber for your help and input.

An enormous thank you to Hannah Holtzer for leading us on the initial design for the book.

Antonia Abramowitz, your exceptional copywriting skills and "get it done" attitude were essential to getting this book published.

Melanie Geller, you were the first one to read this book cover-to-cover and provided great edits and meaningful feedback.

Katie Karas, you made writing my first book a joy-filled experience. You are truly the best editor!

Ann Sawner, thank you for saying "yes" and proofing the entire book! Your brilliance and willingness are a gift to me.

Shannan Buckley, your constant support and outstanding editing skills are deeply appreciated!

ABOUT THE AUTHOR

Eva Wisnik is a career expert and corporate recruiter for America's most prestigious firms. She spent 10 years hiring talent from top schools for investment banks and law firms before launching a very successful search firm in 1996. Eva earned her BA in Psychology from Barnard College, Columbia University and an MBA in Marketing from Fordham University. She is certified in the Myers-Briggs Type Indicator and Covey Time Management System. Her life's mission is to share the secrets for a successful career and fulfilling life with this new generation of young professionals.

www.yourfairyjobmentor.com

Made in the USA
Las Vegas, NV
29 December 2021